LIVING TRUTHS

Living Truths

A Thematic Exposition of Philippians

Danny McCain

AFRICA CHRISTIAN TEXTBOOKS
2012

Living Truths

© 2012 by Danny McCain

Africa Christian Textbooks (ACTS)

ACTS Bookshop, International HQ, TCNN,
PMB 2020, Bukuru, Plateau State, 930008, Nigeria
GSM: +234 (0) 803-589-5328; E-mail: info@acts-ng.com
Website: http://www.acts-ng.com

ISBN: 978-978-905-173-1 Print
ISBN: 978-978-905-262-2 ePub
ISBN: 978-978-905-263-9 Mobi

All rights reserved.

No part of this publication may be reproduced, stored in a retrieval system or transmitted, in any form by any means electronic, mechanical, photocopying, recording or otherwise, without prior permission in writing from the author and the publisher except for brief quotations embodied in articles and reviews.

CONTENTS

PREFACE vii
1. THEMES FROM PHILIPPIANS 1
2. PARTNERSHIP 5
3. PARTNERSHIP 25
4. SUFFERING 43
5. SELFLESSNESS 53
6. HONORABLE CONDUCT 59
7. UNITY 65
8. HUMILITY 77
9. OBEDIENCE 97
10. SERVICE 101
11. CAREFULNESS 111
12. INTIMACY 119
13. SPIRITUAL PROGRESS 131
14. MATURITY 137
15. EXAMPLE 141
16. TRANSFORMATION 147
17. RECONCILIATION 153
18. PRAYER 163
19. OPTIMISM 177
20. CONTENTMENT 193
21. GIVING 199

22. CONCLUSION 207

PREFACE

I have been attracted to the little book of Philippians over the years for several reasons. It is short and simple. It is very personal. And it addresses many of the important themes and issues that the modern Christian faces in life.

I served as the senior pastor of two churches in the US for a total of eight years. During much of that time, I practiced serial expositional preaching in my church. On one occasion, I preached a series of sermons through the Book of Philippians. I took my time and wound up preaching a total of 32 sermons from the book.

After moving from Port Harcourt to Jos in 1991, I began receiving frequent invitations to speak at missions conferences. For some of those I turned to Philippians and discovered that it was an excellent book for missionaries. I am not sure how many times I have preached through Philippians but each time I discovered that it had something new and challenging for the missionaries as well as for me.

On the weekend of February 6-8, 2004, I preached a series of sermons from Philippians to the All Nations Assembly in Kaduna. It was this experience that convinced me that I needed to put these messages into a book. I have been working ever since then to try to do it.

Because the Philippian Church is such a good example of a "missions" church and because this material was presented so many times to missionary audiences, there is a distinct "missionary" flavor in the book. In fact, my primary editor, Dr. Ron Rice, suggested I give the book the title, "Meditations for Missionaries." Though this is one of the rare times when I failed to follow his advice, I do believe this book will provide helpful meditations for missionaries and other Christian workers who read it.

I am grateful for all those who have helped to make this book possible, including those who have heard these oral presentations and encouraged me to publish them. I am most grateful to Dr. Ron Rice for so conscientiously using his bucket of red ink in editing and correcting this book. I am especially grateful to Dr. Sid Garland for pointing out some of the holes in the draft document and suggesting ways to fill them. My wife, Mary, has done her usual excellent job with the tedious final details related to layout, proofreading and checking the accuracy of Biblical quotations. I extend my sincere appreciation to Africa Christian Textbooks (ACTS) for agreeing to publish this book. I am most grateful to God for giving me the privilege of studying and learning and preaching and teaching and taking those things that I have learned and turning them into books.

I pray this book will be as much of a blessing to you in reading it as it has been to me in preparing and writing and preaching it. *"To our God and Father be glory for ever and ever. Amen"* (Philippians 4:20).

Danny McCain
December 2012

CHAPTER 1

THEMES FROM PHILIPPIANS

Introduction

The church at Philippi was a missionary church. The church was one of Paul's missionary success stories—a church planted in a pagan area that grew and flourished. In addition, the congregation at Philippi developed into a missionary sending and supporting church. The church supported Paul as a missionary, in his ongoing ministry of planting additional churches and spreading God's kingdom. The church also sent Epaphroditus to help support Paul do his missionary work.

Thus when we read the Book of Philippians, we are reading about Christian missions at work.

- We see missions on the front end and back end.
- We see the beginning of missions and the maturity of missions.
- We see the birth of a church and we see the birth OF missionaries.
- We see the missionary and the missionary supporter.

Paul first visited the city of Philippi on his second missionary journey (Acts 16:12-40). During that visit, Paul specifically mentions three new converts:

- Lydia, the seller of purple (16:14-15).
- the slave girl from whom the demons were cast out (16:16-18).
- the Philippian jailer (16:27-34).

Though Paul did not stay there more than a few weeks on this first trip, apparently a strong church was established.

We know that Paul revisited the church at least two more times. There is a reasonable possibility that Paul wrote 2 Corinthians from Philippi. Paul continued to have a warm relationship with the Philippian church for the rest of his life. Note the language he used in describing his feelings toward them:

- 1:3, "*I thank my God every time I remember you.*"
- 1:7, "*I have you in my heart . . .*"
- 1:8, "*God can testify how I long for all of you with the affection of Christ Jesus.*"
- 2:12, "*my dear friends*"
- 4:1, "*My brothers, you whom I love and long for, my joy and crown, that is how you should stand firm in the Lord, dear friends!*"

Note also his description of their attitude toward him:

- 2:25, "*Epaphroditus . . . who is also your messenger, whom you sent to take care of my needs.*"
- 4:10, "*I rejoice greatly in the Lord that at last you have renewed your concern for me.*"
- 4:14, "*Yet it was good of you to share in my troubles.*"
- 4:15, "*. . . not one church shared with me in the matter of giving and receiving, except you only . . .*"
- 4:16, "*. . . you sent me aid again and again when I was in need.*"

The Philippians felt especially close to Paul and no doubt became concerned when they found out he had been arrested in Jerusalem and later imprisoned in Rome. They sent one of their church members, Epaphroditus, to Rome to check on Paul and also to help him while he was being detained. Unfortunately, Epaphroditus had gotten sick after arriving, and the news of his sickness had reached the Philippians. Paul decided to send him back to Philippi along with a letter expressing his love and appreciation for them and also giving them some general advice.

> *Paul and Timothy, servants of Christ Jesus, To all the saints in Christ Jesus at Philippi, together with the overseers and deacons: Grace and peace to you from God our Father and the Lord Jesus Christ*
> —Phil. 1:1-2

In the introduction Paul graciously includes Timothy as the co-author. It is not very likely that Timothy actually contributed anything to this epistle. However, it was Paul's practice to include his companions as co-authors of his various epistles. It reinforced the fact that Paul was committed to a team ministry. Even though he was perhaps the greatest leader of the entire Christian era, he realized he needed his ministry companions and this was reflected in the opening lines of his epistles.

Paul also specifically stated that the recipients were *"the saints . . . together with the overseers and deacons."* Paul was writing to all of the believers in Philippi, but, knowing the local customs very well, he specifically mentioned the leaders and workers in the church as the *"overseers and deacons."*

The third part of the introduction is the general greeting. Paul prayed that God's grace and peace would rest upon them. This is a greeting that Paul used in 11 of his 13 epistles. In 1 and 2 Timothy, Paul added a third concept when he greeted them with *"grace, mercy and peace."* In Paul's thinking, all that we experience and enjoy as Christians is due to the grace of God, which should also be reflected in the attitude that we have toward the poor and needy. In addition, perhaps the greatest benefit to the believer of our life in Christ is peace—peace with our conscience, peace with our family, peace with the community, peace with our environment and certainly peace with God.

There is nothing unique about the introduction of Paul's letter to the Philippians. It is similar to the first three or four verses of all Paul's other epistles.

Because Philippians is a missionary book, a careful study will provide insights for all who are interested in missions, including those who go as missionaries and those who stay behind and support missionaries from their homes. That should include practically all Christian believers. Because of the missionary nature of the book, I speak directly to missionaries some times and, in fact, it might sound like a missionary book.

In this book, I will be looking at a number of themes and principles from Philippians roughly in the order in which they appear. This is not an exhaustive commentary on the Book of Philippians but is what I call thematic exposition. I will not attempt to address every theme or topic or even every verse in the book but will attempt to address the major themes as they naturally develop throughout the book.

It is my prayer that the missionary spirit that was part of the lives of both the writer and recipients of this epistle will become a part of everyone who reads this book.

CHAPTER 2

PARTNERSHIP

Paul's Relationship with the Philippians (1:3-18)

The key phrase in the first paragraph is found in 1:4, *"your partnership in the gospel."* The word translated "partnership" here is the Greek *koinonia*. In classical Greek it had the idea of association or participation or that which was shared in common with others. For example, public property was the land that was shared in common by all the citizens of a state.

In the New Testament, *koinonia* is the word that is used to describe the unique relationship between believers. They are like a body. They share many things in common. They work together and need one another and spend time with one another in order to fulfill their individual duties.

Body Parts Are Partners

The members of my body are all partners. They work very wonderfully together. While I am typing this sentence, many things are happening: My legs have brought my body and placed it in a position where it can reach the computer. My backbone is holding my body erect so I can see the computer. My brain is thinking about the words that need to be used to communicate properly. My eyes are looking at the computer screen to make sure the right words get in the right place. My fingers are typing away at the keys. My arms are holding my hands in place. And my stomach is impatiently waiting for some breakfast. I would say that qualifies the members of my body to be partners in this writing project.

A partnership is normally thought of as a project by two or more individuals where there is joint ownership, joint privileges and joint duties. When the missionaries first came to Nigeria, they planted churches and supervised them for many years. It was primarily a father-son type of relationship. Missionaries were in charge of the schools, the hospitals and the church administration. Eventually the control of the churches and schools and other institutions was handed over to the Nigerians. In some cases, the missionaries left. In other cases, the missionaries remained and became subservient to their Nigerian counterparts. In other cases, a partnership was created. The mission and the church work together as equal partners on certain projects. One does not dominate the other. They make decisions jointly and enjoy equal privileges and equal responsibilities.

By using the concept of partnership, Paul was declaring that the Philippians were not just his spiritual subjects. They were partners together in the ministry of spreading the gospel. Paul wrote, *"All of you share in God's grace . . ."* (1:7b). This reflects something of the maturity of the Philippian church. It also certainly reflects the maturity and humility of Paul in declaring that his converts were not his subjects but were now his partners.

In this section, we will look at this special partner relationship from Paul's point of view. This represents the relationship of the missionary with his or her supporting church. In the next chapter, we will look at the partnership from the viewpoint of the local Philippian church.

Paul's Attitude toward the Philippians

Paul's attitude toward the Philippians is demonstrated in three positive results.

An Attitude of Thankfulness

Paul began *"I thank my God every time I remember you"* (1:3). Paul had a spirit of gratefulness toward those who had assisted him with the ministry. He recognized that his ministry would be impossible without the other members of the body of Christ. The Philippians were helping to make Paul's ministry possible. Therefore, Paul was thankful.

The Christian worker today who receives at least some of his or her financial support from the church must be a grateful recipient. We must always have a spirit of gratefulness toward those who make it possible for us to be involved in ministry.

This spirit of gratefulness is just as important today as it was in Paul's day. Not only should we feel grateful, we should express that gratefulness as often and in as many ways as we can. Those of us involved in ministry must express our gratitude regularly to those who assist us in the ministry. We must be grateful for many things.

- We must be grateful for the trust given us to represent a part of the body of Christ.
- We must be grateful for the funds that others supply to us that make our ministry possible.
- We must be grateful for those who pray for us.
- We must be grateful for those who come to visit us and encourage and support us.
- We must be grateful to those who write letters and send emails.

- We must be grateful for those family members who help take up some of our family duties.
- We must be grateful for those who do the tedious administrative tasks in order to free us up to do the things that we do best.

Saying "thank you" is the cheapest and most effective form of public relations one can use. I will tell two brief stories that illustrate that point.

A Note of Thanks

Some time ago, I was cleaning up my office and I ran across a pink piece of paper that had been torn out of a spiral notebook. I remembered that this piece of paper with ragged edges was handed to me in a board meeting many years ago by one of the board members of the International Institute for Christian Studies. It simply said, "Danny: Thanks for having the dream. Floyd 1/29/93." That note was handed to me well over a decade ago but I still have it. Why? Because someone said thank you in a very simple but meaningful manner. He appreciated the vision that God had given to me in helping to establish the organization. That pink piece of paper still reminds me of that humble spirit of gratefulness that was demonstrated that day.

The Pain of Not Saying Thank You

In 1976, my senior son, Nathaniel, got sick with spinal meningitis and, after five days, he died. Normally, in the American culture, one of the ways we express our sympathy to those who lose loved ones is to give or send flowers to the family of the bereaved. Because few people have the necessary flowers in their garden to make up an appropriate bouquet, providing flowers for funerals has become a big commercial enterprise. Often there are literally thousands of dollars' worth of flowers at a funeral service. Since flowers usually fade and die in a few days, some Christian organizations have encouraged people to show their sympathy to families by donating the money that would have been spent on flowers to a charity or a church or a mission in the name of the deceased. In this way, some part of the body of Christ would benefit from the sympathy that was being expressed.

As a practical minded person, I have been sympathetic toward this alternative way of showing sympathy. When my son died, I designated a certain missionary organization as one that I would like to see gifts given in the name of my son. I do not know how much if any money was given to that organization in honor of my son. However, I do know this: no one from that organization ever said one word of thanks to me for what we had attempted to do. Perhaps they were too busy; perhaps they did not know the best way to say thanks; perhaps they forgot, but I know that I have not forgotten. I am neither angry nor unforgiving. However, I know it was painful to me that no one even acknowledged the fact that in the time when I was hurting the most, I had thought about them. And I still remember that hurt 35 years later.

I seldom ever write a letter or email to anyone without saying thank you in some kind of different way than I have said it before. Every time I am in the US, I try to make a phone call to those people who donate money regularly to our ministry. It is amazing how often I notice another gift from that person the next month after my phone call. We should not just say thank you as a gimmick to get more money. We should say thank you out of a genuine heart of gratitude. However, one of the best ways to keep our friends supporting our ministries is to say thank you regularly and sincerely.

The most important strategy of raising funds in our organization is saying thank you. We follow up every gift with a thank-you letter within 24 hours of the time it is received. In certain cases, someone phones the donor to say thank you personally.

My challenge to every pastor and missionary and Christian worker is that you develop and maintain not only a spirit of gratefulness but a plan to make sure that gratefulness is communicated to your partners in ministry.

An Attitude of Prayer

When we think of prayer and mission work, we normally think of the sending body praying for the person who is sent. However, in this case, the Philippians not only prayed for Paul, Paul prayed for them as well. Paul wrote *"In all my prayers for all of you, I always pray with joy because of your partnership in the gospel..."* (1:4-5).

The fact Paul prayed for the Philippians implied that there was a personal relationship between him and the church. He had not just gone to the church to recruit staff or raise funds but he actually had a personal relationship with them. Thus he could pray intelligently about the needs of the church.

Being able to pray intelligently for a person or church or ministry implies something of a relationship with that person, church or organization. It is important for Christian workers to spend some time with the people who are supporting their ministry so they get to know them.

Our organization adds several people to our staff every year. I am normally sent their CV's. I receive all the notes from the interview process. After they are sent to a university somewhere around the world, I receive their newsletters and other information that tells me about their ministry. Unfortunately, I really do not know them and, frankly, it is quite hard to get excited about their ministries or even pray for them. However, whenever I am able to meet them usually at our annual conference, I develop a relationship with them and that helps me to know better how to pray for them.

Let us make sure that we are not only the recipients of the prayers of those who support our ministry but we are praying for them as well.

An Attitude of Love

Paul continued, "*I have you in my heart . . .*" (1:7). He added in the next verse, "*God can testify how I long for all of you with the affection of Christ Jesus.*" Paul had planted the church in Philippi and therefore had something of a fatherly relationship with them. However, love really does not develop well at a distance. The reason Paul loved them was that he had spent significant time with them. He had a good relationship with them.

The word translated "*affection*" in the NIV is the Greek *splagchnon* which literally refers to a person's intestines. It was obviously an idiom that was used to describe the positive emotion of love. In our modern world, we tend to describe the emotions of a person as coming from the heart. However, in the ancient world, other internal organs were used to illustrate the source of emotions including kidneys (Job 16:13; 19:27; Psalm 7:9; 16:7; Proverbs 23:16; Isaiah 11:5; Jeremiah 11:20; Revelation 2:23) and intestines or bowels (Genesis 43:30; 1 Kings 3:26; Job 30:27; Psalm 22:14; Jeremiah 31:20; Colossians 3:12; 1 John 3:17). The NIV and most modern translations remove the idiom and simply translate this word "affection."

This particular idiom describes the strong emotional attachment that Jesus demonstrated for his people (Matthew 9:36; 14:14; 15:32; 20:34; Mark 1:41). Jesus is the epitome of love. According to my count, the word "love" is associated with Jesus at least 38 times in the New Testament. Since a Christian is a follower of Jesus, then perhaps the first and most important characteristic that we must have is love. Paul loved the Philippians with the "affection of Christ." We must have that same kind of affection if we are to be true followers of Christ.

This focus on love is another indication that the missionary and the missionary sending body should have a close and warm relationship with one another.

Churches fund various missionaries and missionary organizations in different ways. However funding is done, there needs to be a good link between the missionaries and the home team so that a good relationship can develop between the two. There can be no true partnership without good relationships.

All missionaries and other Christian workers who are supported by the gifts of God's people must ask themselves the question: Does my attitude toward those who support my ministry reflect the idea of partnership?

Paul's Prayer for the Philippians (1:9-11)

If you were to ask Mr. Joe Missionary what he would like to see happen in his supporting churches, he would probably say he would love to see them prosper financially so that they could give more money to his ministry. This is not necessarily a bad desire. It obviously takes money for any ministry to fulfill its mission. However, this was not Paul's first desire for the Philippian church. His primary desire and prayer for the church was that they would prosper spiritually.

> *And this is my prayer: that your love may abound more and more in knowledge and depth of insight, so that you may be able to discern what is best and may be pure and blameless until the day of Christ, filled with the fruit of righteousness that comes through Jesus Christ —to the glory and praise of God.*
> —Phil. 1:9-11

Note the specific things Paul desired for the Philippian church:

- *They would increase in love; "that your love may abound more and more"* (1:9a). Somewhere near the heart of Christianity is the concept of selfless and giving love.
- *They would expand their knowledge; "in knowledge"* (1:9b). Christianity is based upon truth which is the correct knowledge. Therefore, the true Christian is a learning Christian.
- *They would increase in wisdom; "so that you may be able to discern what is best"* (1:10a). Learning eventually produces insight or wisdom in one's life. Wisdom is the ability to use knowledge to make good decisions.
- *They would become pure and blameless; "may be pure and blameless"* (1:10b). The ethical side of Christianity is purity in the heart and blamelessness in the life.
- *They would bear the fruit of righteousness; "filled with the fruit of righteousness"* (1:11a). The word righteousness in this context refers to right living. The love and knowledge and wisdom that the believer has will eventually produce right living in his or her life which is another way of describing the blamelessness of the previous phrase. This is a kind of righteousness that comes from Christ and is patterned after his own righteous life.
- *They would bring honor and glory to God; "to the glory and praise of God"* (1:11b). Obviously, everything in our lives is designed to be a positive credit to God. We must live in such a way that when people see us they glorify our Father in heaven (Matthew 5:16).

It is obvious that Paul was just as concerned about the spiritual welfare of the Philippians as he was concerned about the people he was trying to reach in Rome. From his place of detention in Rome, he was concerned about evangelism, but in Philippi, Paul was concerned about their ongoing maturity, discipleship and sanctification.

This prayer suggests that missionaries have something to contribute to those churches that support them. Unfortunately, most of the time when missionaries have the opportunity to speak at their sponsoring churches, they have to spend a lot of time reporting on the work of God in their ministry. This is right and proper and one of the points I will stress next. However, it is unfortunate that most of the time this missionary who has gained great insight into the Bible and human nature has very few opportunities to truly minister to those back home. Paul's example is a challenge to all missionaries to make sure they share more than just "thank you's" with those who support them.

Paul's Report to the Philippians (1:12)

Paul felt that one of his responsibilities was to report to his supporting churches. He began the next section, *"Now I want you to know, brothers . . ."* and then proceeded to give the church a summary of his activities.

Reporting to the sponsoring body, the mother church, was an important principle in the early church. When Peter had the amazing experience with Cornelius, he went straight back to Jerusalem, assembled the church leaders, and reported to them what had happened (Acts 11:1-18). Paul and Barnabas were sent on their first missionary journey by the church at Antioch. The Holy Spirit directed the church to set apart Barnabas and Saul (Paul), so they laid hands on them and sent them out. At the end of that first missionary journey we read:

> *From Attalia they sailed back to Antioch, where they had been committed to the grace of God for the work they had now completed. On arriving there, they gathered the church together and reported all that God had done through them, and how he had opened the door of faith to the Gentiles.*
>
> —Acts 14:26-27

When Paul completed his second missionary journey, he also returned to Antioch and reported to the church. No doubt Paul intended to go back to Antioch and report to the church after his third missionary trip but he was prohibited from doing so by his arrest in Jerusalem.

Why should we report to our sponsors?

Reporting is common in business, education, government and most professional organizations. Why do these entities require reporting?

- Reporting to one's sponsors is morally right. If other people have invested money or energy or prayers in a project they have a right to know as much about that project as they desire.
- Reporting to one's sponsors will help improve the relationship between those who sponsor projects and those who implement them. The reports should contain the kinds of information that will help sponsors to understand the personality, character and style of leadership that the field person brings to the project.
- Reporting to one's sponsors helps the sponsors to pray more intelligently for the ministries they support.
- Reporting to one's sponsors is an important part of the monitoring and evaluation that should be part of all projects. To be able to report properly means that those implementing the projects have done a proper assessment and evaluation.

What should we report to our sponsors?

Paul reported good things God was doing.

There is no particular place in Philippians that Paul specifically states this. However, this was his practice when he returned to the church at Antioch. He gathered the church together and *"reported all that God had* done through them and how he had opened the door of faith to the Gentiles" (Acts 14:27b). God's people are always happy to hear what God is doing. Our reports are testimonies to God's goodness and work. They are proofs to those who have invested their funds that their investments are worthwhile.

"Projects We Are Doing"

When we go back to the USA, we always go to Melbourne, Florida and visit one of the board members of the International Institute for Christian Studies. It makes me feel good to hear him talk about the ministry of our organization. He always uses first person pronouns. "God is blessing *our* projects . . . this is what *we* are doing . . . if you have any questions talk to *us*." Although he has never been to Africa, he believes correctly that he is a vital part of our ministry. He can make those statements because he gets good reports and those reports help him feel a part of the ministry.

A Special Honor

On January 24, 1996, I was invited to open the US Congress in prayer. Twelve hours before this, the president of the United States had stood in the same spot and given his State of the Union address. This was obviously a special privilege. I was raised in a pietistic movement where we were taught that you do not talk about yourself very much. Doing so may encourage pride. Therefore, I was a little hesitant to tell people about this special honor. However, in a phone conversation with one of my good friends who had heard about this, he got very excited about it and demanded that I tell him about every detail. His happiness made me happy so I decided to tell another friend. This person was just as excited and when we closed our conversation, he said, "And, Danny, thanks a lot for telling me about the prayer in congress." That experience helped me to understand that when I receive a blessing, it is also a blessing to my family and all those who are close to me. Since that time, I have tried to be more open about the good things that come my way.

Blessings we have received in our ministry are a benefit to the whole ministry team. Do not deprive the other team members of the blessings that your ministry is receiving by keeping them to yourself.

Paul reported hardships and difficulties.

Paul's prison experience was not the greatest success story of his missionary career. However, he was very upfront in reporting it to the Philippians.

> *Now I want you to know, brothers, that what has happened to me has really served to advance the gospel. As a result, it has become clear throughout the whole palace guard and to everyone else that I am in chains for Christ. Because of my chains, most of the brothers in the Lord have been encouraged to speak the word of God more courageously and fearlessly.*
>
> —Phil. 1:12-14

"All missionaries are liars." This is a statement I make at times to stress this point. I find that most missionaries and other people serving overseas, including myself, tend to report only the good things. I enjoy talking about the successful things we have experienced in our ministry, the teaching and preaching and seminars and counseling and writings and other things that will make people feel good and convince them the money they are investing in this ministry is being used well.

However, I was convicted some years ago that I was not properly reflecting the reality of our ministry in Nigeria. Our organization had encountered some serious difficulties that I had said nothing about. Because our friends knew nothing about these things, they could not help us pray about them or share with us any wisdom and experience that they may have gained in those areas.

I encourage missionaries to report honestly to their supporters. Tell them the good and the bad. Be balanced in your reporting. Do not be overly optimistic or pessimistic but realistic in the things you share with those who support your ministry.

Very few of us like to give or hear negative reports. Unfortunately, it is necessary to give such reports at times. Therefore, when it is necessary to report negative things, try to apply these guidelines:

Do not dwell on it. Notice that Paul said little or nothing about his imprisonment throughout the rest of the epistle. He mentioned the prison experience so they would be informed and know how to pray but this was not the theme of his letter.

Focus on the positive. Even when negative things happen to us, the eye of faith will see that God is using them in a positive way. Note the many good things Paul pointed out just in this section that were happening because of his imprisonment:

- It had advanced the gospel (1:12).
- It had spread throughout the whole palace guard (1:13).
- It had encouraged many of the brothers to speak the word of God boldly (1:14).

There are certainly positive ways of reporting negative things. We do not want people to get the impression that the missionaries are poor, miserable people for whom others should feel sorry. That is not the impression you get when reading Paul's report to the Philippian believers. Most missionaries feel very fortunate to be serving in their respective places of ministry, even when they face difficulties. However, those who support the ministry from their home lands need to be properly and holistically informed so they can pray intelligently.

Paul reported his goals.

> Not that I have already obtained all this, or have already been made perfect, but I press on to take hold of that for which Christ Jesus took hold of me. Brothers, I do not consider myself yet to have taken hold of it. But one thing I do: Forgetting what is behind and straining toward what is ahead, I press toward the goal to win the prize for which God has called me heavenward in Christ Jesus.
> —Phil. 3:12-14

Here Paul outlines some of his spiritual goals. Although he couches this with an athletic metaphor, he is simply saying his goal is to fulfill God's will for his life. God had called him for a purpose. He was grateful for the progress he had made to this point but he was not satisfied to remain at one place. He wanted to continue finding ways to fulfill what God had called him to do.

Although Paul does not specifically outline his ministry goals, they are hinted at in his personal goals. God had called him to win the Gentiles for Christ. That was certainly one of his most important goals. The fact Paul shared his goals with the Philippians suggests the importance of missionaries sharing goals with those supporting them.

- What has God called you to do?
- What are you trying to do in your ministry?
- What do you want to accomplish during the next year?
- What are the long-range goals of your ministry?

Before we can share our goals with others, we need to think through our goals ourselves. We need to take time to think about the direction our ministry is going. We need to build times of reflection and planning into our schedules.

Paul's Ministry to the Philippians

Not only did Paul minister to the people in the mission field, he still maintained a ministry to those who were supporting him. He was involved in several different kinds of ministry.

Exhortation

Paul wrote, "*Whatever happens, conduct yourselves in a manner worthy of the gospel of Christ*" (1:27). In the next chapter he wrote,

> *Therefore, my dear friends, as you have always obeyed—not only in my presence, but now much more in my absence—continue to work out your salvation with fear and trembling.*
> —Phil. 2:12

Paul felt a responsibility not only to represent this church as their missionary; he also felt the need to encourage and exhort them. Would it not be good for pastors and churches to give missionaries a chance to speak to them and exhort them on things other than missions?

Warning

In 3:2, Paul wrote, "*Watch out for those dogs, those men who do evil, those mutilators of the flesh.*" This was a warning against the Jewish Christians who stressed the importance of circumcision. Having served God in many places, Paul was able to see the dangers that the Philippians faced from a much different perspective than they were able to see. Therefore, he used his experience and insight into the nature of the enemy to warn the Philippians about the pitfalls they would face.

If there is the proper relationship between the missionary and the supporting church, there should be opportunities for that missionary to share exhortations and warnings that could help the congregation not only give more money to missions but improve their own spiritual welfare.

Example

"Join with others in following my example, brothers, and take note of those who live according to the pattern we gave you" (3:17). One of the most important things missionaries can do for the people in their supporting churches is to be good examples. The people know that most missionaries make sacrifices. However, when they go back with cheerful hearts and grateful attitudes and the joy of the Lord, those characteristics encourage those in their home churches to be more committed and sacrificial.

The Example of a College President

When I was attending a Christian college, I traveled with a musical group from that institution. One day we visited Dr. Dale Yocum, the president of another Christian college that was well known to us. He had boxes piled up in his living room. Dr. Yocum was packing his possessions to go as a missionary to Korea.

That event made a very powerful impression on me. Here was a man who had reached the pinnacle of success. At that point in my life, becoming the president of a Christian college seemed to be the ultimate success for a Christian leader. And now this man was putting aside all of that to go to the mission field. Dr. Dale Yocum served in Korea for 10 years before returning to the US.

Over the years, Dr. Yocum continued to have a very profound impact on my life and probably had as much influence on pushing me toward serving God overseas as anyone else. This godly man died shortly before I moved to Nigeria, but his example still inspires me and influences the ministry God has given me.

Problem Solving

Paul wrote, "*I plead with Euodia and I plead with Syntyche to agree with each other in the Lord*" (4:2). There was an interpersonal problem in the Philippian church that needed to be solved. Because Paul was one of the founders of the church and a recognized worldwide Christian leader, he used his influence to help bring reconciliation between these two Christian ladies. Even though evangelism and church planting were important to him, preserving the unity of a local church was also important.

Sometimes the missionary can be the ideal person to help solve interpersonal problems in a church. He or she should be far enough removed from the situation to be objective, yet close enough to the church to be able to aid in reconciliation and restoration.

Summary

Paul's comments demonstrate clearly that the person who is sent should have a ministry to those who are sending. The most obvious ministry is providing those from the sending church the opportunity to give financial support to the work of the Great Commission. However, that should not be the only ministry to the supporters. As God gives them opportunity, missionaries can also be involved in many of the same things as Paul: exhorting, warning, problem solving and being an example.

I used to feel sorry for missionaries for one main reason. Every time a missionary came to our church, we always sang the same mission hymns.

> *We have heard the joyful sound; Jesus Saves! Jesus Saves!*
> *Spread the tidings all around; Jesus Saves! Jesus Saves!*
> *Bear the news to every land; Climb the steeps and cross the waves;*
> *Onward!—'tis our Lord's command; Jesus Saves! Jesus Saves!*

Another song we like to sing whenever the missionaries visited us was:

> *Rescue the perishing; Care for the dying; Snatch them in pity from sin and the grave.*
> *Weep o'er the erring one, Lift up the fallen; Tell them of Jesus, the mighty to save.*
> *Rescue the perishing; Care for the dying; Jesus is merciful; Jesus will save.*

I am sure those missionaries heard that same set of hymns in every other church they visited! I am sure missionaries would love to hear some of the other wonderful hymns of the church. Thus, as a pastor, whenever I invited a missionary to our church, I deliberately refused to sing the traditional missionary songs.

However, after serving God in Nigeria for 24 years, I now feel sorry for missionaries for a second reason—because they have to make the same fund raising speech every place they go. Missionaries are rich in experience and wisdom and knowledge of the Bible. Of course, we recognize the importance of reporting as I have discussed earlier. It would also be wonderful if missionaries could have an opportunity to minister in a broader way to the people who assist them rather than just making the same kind of reporting speech all the time.

Paul had an outstanding relationship with the Philippians, one that is a model for our churches and missionaries to emulate today.

CHAPTER 3

PARTNERSHIP

The Philippians' Relationship with Paul (1:19; 2:25; 4:15-19)[1]

Not only is it important to see the kind of relationship that Paul had with the Philippians, it is equally important to see what kind of relationship the Philippians had with Paul. What were the things that the Philippians did or provided for Paul?

Prayer Support

Paul wrote,

> For I know that through your prayers and the help given me by the Spirit of Jesus Christ, what has happened to me will turn out for my deliverance.
>
> —Phil. 1:19

---

[1] As a general rule, thematic exposition should follow the normal progression of the passage, a paragraph at a time in the order in which the thoughts occur. However, I have chosen to include observations about the Philippian's relationship to Paul from several parts of the book at this point because they fit logically with the Paul's relationship with the Philippians, which is the major theme of the first half of this chapter.

Paul was very certain the Philippians' prayers were critical if God were to deliver him from prison.

The most important thing a supporting church can do for missionaries is to pray for them.

- Whether you have money or not, you can pray.
- Whether you know the missionary or not, you can pray.
- Whether you are able to visit the mission field or not, you can pray.

Why should you pray for your missionaries?

Missionaries cannot always pray for themselves.

Missionaries tend to be very busy people. They often have people in their homes. When people are waiting to see you in the sitting room or office, it is hard to concentrate on prayer. The missionary often has many responsibilities. He or she can work from early until late and there will still be unfinished tasks. This also hinders prayer. Though I am not attempting to excuse the missionary from praying, I believe at times God accepts the prayers of other people on the missionary's behalf.

Sometimes missionaries are in danger and there is not enough time for them to alert others to pray.

We need to pray daily for our missionaries. However, we also need to be sensitive to the leadership of the Spirit who may encourage us to pray for a person at a certain time. Very often that person needs prayer desperately at a specific time.

God Speaks at a Distance

In 2001 we had a severe crisis in Jos in which there was much ethnic and religious violence. For several days we observed the smoke from burning buildings, heard the gunfire of the battle, took care of dozens of refugees and sympathized with those who had lost property and loved ones. There was very limited movement during that time and also very limited communication with the outside world.

My oldest daughter, Carmen, who was living in New York City at the time, heard about the crisis and wrote us an email pleading to hear from us. She also sent a copy of the same email to some of our relatives, along with an article about the ongoing crisis in Jos. A few days later, I received the following note from my brother-in-law who is a roofing contractor in Florida.

> We were in tears Sunday morning when I opened my e-mail from Carmen and read her plea to hear from you soon about your safety. I felt a strange feeling come over me as I read about the violence there. I could not believe what I was reading. Just the day before, on Saturday about 2-3 in the afternoon I was sitting in our back porch, listening to soft music and meditating and praying. I looked out over our back yard and into the distance and started feeling a strange feeling. I suddenly felt that you were in danger. I was looking at the university area and down the streets and back to your house. I felt that violence and killing were going on. It was like I was in a trance. I am happy some of the sights I was seeing did not happen, since Danny is OK. I was a little terrified at what I was seeing happening to Danny, and I breathed a prayer.

God had inspired my brother-in-law to pray for me at a very critical time. All of us need to be sensitive to pray for missionaries and others as the Lord prompts us.

Sometimes missionaries have needs they cannot solve with their own resources or ingenuity.

When a person goes to another culture, there are problems of adjustment, language learning, culture learning, and difficulties with the food, the water and other challenges. There is seldom a day when the missionary does not have problems. If you have no particular burden to pray for the missionary, that does not mean there are no problems. Missionaries always have problems and need prayer.

We should pray for our missionaries because we believe God answers our prayers.

James wrote, *"The prayer of a righteous man is powerful and effective"* (5:16b). The KJV translates this: *"The effectual fervent prayer of a righteous man availeth much."* Jesus said,

> *So I say to you: Ask and it will be given to you; seek and you will find; knock and the door will be opened to you. For everyone who asks receives; he who seeks finds; and to him who knocks, the door will be opened. Which of you fathers, if your son asks for a fish, will give him a snake instead? Of if he asks for an egg, will give him a scorpion? If you then, though you are evil, know how to give good gifts to your children, how much more will your Father in heaven give the Holy Spirit to those who ask him!.*
> —Luke 11:9-13

There are dozens of Scriptures that promise God will answer our prayers. It is an amazing thought, that God Almighty, the maker of heaven and earth, would even hear our prayers, much less take time out of his busy schedule to answer them.

How should you pray for your missionaries?

You should pray regularly.

Do not pray for missionaries only as you think about them but pray daily or regularly. If we pray only as we remember them, we will not pray often. Most of us are so busy we do not have the leisure of thinking about things that are not necessary.

It is good for every church to schedule regular prayer meetings to pray for missionary projects the local church supports. It would be a great source of encouragement for missionaries to know that at least once every week a particular person or church was praying for them.

You should pray intelligently.

The Philippians made a special effort to get to know Paul and his specific needs. This helped them to pray intelligently for Paul.

This suggests we should learn as much about the various missionaries we support as possible. Become familiar with their strengths and weaknesses. Read their emails and prayer letters.

You should pray specifically.

All missionaries have certain problems such as cultural adjustment, loneliness, limited contact with their families, financial shortfalls, overwork, and similar problems. All missionaries also have specific problems that arise related to their ministry. Learn about what the particular needs are and pray for them. Do not pray, "Lord, remember all the missionaries in the world." Pray, "Lord, Brother John Bulus is preaching in a missionary conference tomorrow. Assist him in his preparation. Give him exactly what this congregation needs. Help him to speak with passion and conviction and may his sermon bear fruit so that 10 people will respond to go to the mission field as a result of his sermon."

Most missionaries have families. Pray for the families by name. One of my former pastors sends me emails occasionally. In nearly every email he will say, "Danny, I want to remind you that I pray for you and Mary and your children by name every day." Nothing my former pastor could say to me is more meaningful than that. It would be a special gift to give to your missionary families the commitment to pray for them and each member of their families by name every day.

You should pray fervently.

I still prefer the KJV version of James 5:16, "The effectual fervent prayer of a righteous man availeth much." Fervent praying is serious prayer. It is more than just a passing thought through the mind. Fervent praying may involve fasting or may involve an extended period of time. Fervent prayer is a characteristic of those who are giants in their faith—who recognize that God appreciates and responds to the prayers of his people.

You should pray as you are led by the Spirit.

Paul wrote:

> We do not know what we ought to pray for, but the Spirit himself intercedes for us with groans that words cannot express. And he who searches our hearts knows the mind of the Spirit, because the Spirit inter-cedes for the saints in accordance with God's will.
> —Romans 8:26-27

at times things that we need to pray about. We should be listening to the voice of the Spirit in our lives. The Spirit knows all of the circumstances of life and is very capable of prompting us to pray about specific needs.

The point is that we need to be sensitive to the leadership of the Holy Spirit who at times gently nudges us to pray.

You should pray creatively.

We normally think of praying for missionaries as something we do when we are praying quietly or in groups. However, there are other things you can do to make sure that you pray for missionaries.

1. *Have a missionary prayer list.* I have a prayer list of about eight pages with the names of missionaries and missionary organizations that I pray for. The list is too long for me to pray for daily so I try to pray for this long list on Mondays.
2. *Write out prayers.* On May 31, 2002, we received an email from a good friend in our home church in the USA. At the end of the email, our friend wrote out a prayer for us, specifically mentioning issues that were coming up in our lives:

   > Heavenly Father we thank you so much for your loving hand of protection on Mary and Danny. We thank you that your grace is sufficient for each day we face. I lift up Mary, and ask you to help her to prioritize the things she must get done and help her to not feel stress over all that lies before her in preparing for their trip. Lord, I pray you will give Mary a clear mind to proofread Danny's book for him and that she would not feel rushed or distracted. Help her to prepare her home for anyone who may stay there. Please protect them while they travel and make their journey pleasant. I thank you for bringing them home to their church family and I pray that our time together will glorify you.

As far as I know, that was the first email prayer we had ever received. I have been writing out prayers for many years in my devotional journal.

However, I learned something from this. I want to make sure that I write out prayers for my friends also. Yes our prayers are to God but it is good for others to see what we are praying to God.

Prayer is something all of us can do. We do not have to have a computer to write out a prayer and send it to someone. I think that receiving a prayer which you took time to write out and send would be a great blessing to your missionaries. It would assure them that you are seriously praying for them.

You may not be able to do a lot for your missionaries. However, one thing every one of us can do is to pray for them. James wrote, *"You do not have, because you do not ask God"* (4:2). Let us not be guilty of not asking for our missionaries.

Personnel Support

> *But I think it is necessary to send back to you Epaphroditus, my brother, fellow worker, and fellow soldier, who is also your messenger, whom you sent to take care of my needs.*
> —Philippians 2:25

When the Philippian church heard that Paul was imprisoned in Rome, their first thought was to help him. He needed two types of help, some financial support, and someone to assist him with some of the practical details. Therefore they took up an offering and sent a brother named Epaphroditus to help him.

Paul only had positive words of praise for Epaphroditus. Unfortunately, he had gotten sick and had almost died. Thankfully, he had recovered but Paul knew the Philippian brothers and sisters were concerned about his health, so he sent Epaphroditus back to them along with the Philippian letter.

Churches can help recruit personnel in many ways:

The church should recruit long-term staff to go to the mission field.

The pastor should regularly remind the church of their duty to missions. Missionary work should be regularly featured in the prayer requests. There should be regular services to focus attention on missionary work. The church should turn visits of missionaries into special occasions. The missionary should be honored highly in our churches so that our young people will grow up to admire and respect them. In other words, missionary work should receive a prominent focus in the church.

Providing scholarships and encouraging university-age young people to attend mission conferences is an excellent way for a church to interest young people in missionary work at a critical time in their lives, when they are making decisions about their future. Churches should also appeal to those reaching retirement age to consider using their skills on the mission field.

There is probably nothing that would help your missionary more than recruiting someone who would go and serve with him or her on a full-time, long-term basis.

The church should recruit short-term people to assist in missionary work.

God does not call everyone to go to the mission field on a long-term basis. However, he does call everyone to be interested in missions. One of the ways that a local church can get their people more involved in missions is to get them to go to the mission field and work on a specific project.

Short Term Missions Trips

When I was 18 years old, I attended a school in southern Florida. A missionary, who worked in the Bahamas about 100 kilometers away, would frequently visit our school. He convinced me to go to the Bahamas to help him paint some buildings. One weekend I flew over with two other friends to help "paint the mission" and do some other practical work that the missionary said he did not have time to do. We discovered that the painting job was not as urgent as we had thought. The missionary had just used the painting as an excuse to get us exposed to the mission field.

Later, shortly after we were married, my wife and I went to a mission station in the Turks and Caicos Islands for two weeks to substitute for a missionary family so they could return home for Christmas. It was those early exposures to the mission field that created an interest in me to go overseas to serve Christ.

Short-term mission trips can be easily abused. Most of us have heard stories of short-term helpers who got in the way more than they helped out. Short-term missionaries never want to become a burden to the missionary they are trying to help. Therefore, short-term missionary trips must be planned with the full participation and enthusiasm of the host missionary.

When we lived in Port Harcourt, a friend from the US spent a week with us. He went through the house and repaired everything that was broken, including spoiled clocks, faulty electrical outlets, plumbing problems and vehicle problems. He even helped to tune our piano. This friend was a true blessing and his type of short-term missionary is welcome at my house any time.

I doubt if there is a better way church members could encourage and help their missionaries than recruiting and sending people to assist them.

Financial Support

> *Moreover, as you Philippians know, in the early days of your acquaintance with the gospel, when I set out from Macedonia, not one church shared with me in the matter of giving and receiving, except you only; for even when I was in Thessalonica, you sent me aid again and again when I was in need. Not that I am looking for a gift, but I am looking for what may be credited to your account. . . . I have received from Epaphroditus the gifts you sent. They are a fragrant offering, an acceptable sacrifice, pleasing to God. And my God will meet all your needs according to his glorious riches in Christ Jesus.*
> —Philippians 4:15-19

The Philippian church had given more financial aid to Paul than any other church. Paul promised that God would meet all their needs, *"according to his glorious riches in Christ Jesus."*

We love this promise but have we ever noticed that the promise comes in the context of giving? The reason God was going to meet all their needs was because they had been faithful to give to others. If we want God to supply all our needs, we need to make sure we are regularly giving to God's causes.

Few missionaries can go to the mission field without the financial support of the church. God does call some missionaries to be tent makers. Like the Apostle Paul, these people have an occupation which enables them to make their living and do ministry simultaneously. Though we are grateful for these people, God calls many people to be full time in the work of the Lord. And when God calls such people, he calls other people to support them.

Would you like to know what the hardest job for the missionary is? It is not learning a new language, or learning to eat strange kinds of food, or adjusting to a different culture or climate. It is raising funds. Many missionaries are very good at what they do. They are excellent missionaries but poor fundraisers. I encourage those involved in raising money in the church for missionaries to do all they can to free the missionary from this responsibility. Missionaries do not mind testifying about their work. In fact, they love to tell people about what God is doing in their ministry. However, being responsible to raise the necessary money to keep themselves on the field often makes them feel like beggars. Most missionaries do not mind raising money for missions but they do not like to raise money for themselves.

If God's people are going to work full time on a specific project, that means they are going to have to have others support them. It is essential for the body of Christ to donate large sums of money to help those whom God has called to do full time Christian ministry. Remember that the missionary is making a lot of sacrifices. Many of the missionaries that your churches support gave up the possibility of pursuing very lucrative careers in order to go into missions where they have to raise money for their own support. Please remember:

- Missionaries have families to care for.
- Missionaries have school fees to pay.
- Missionaries have financial responsibilities to extended family members.
- Missionaries have many travel expenses.
- Missionaries have a lot of people who look to them to help with other needs.
- Missionaries have expenses related to their ministry.

I encourage local churches to take good care of their missionaries. It is true that missionaries should be making sacrifices. However, let them make their own voluntary sacrifices and be rewarded for it. Do not make those sacrifices for them.

A Model for Supporting Christian Workers

Jacob's 12 sons became the founders of the 12 tribes. Joseph, one of Jacob's sons, had two sons, Ephraim and Manasseh. Each of these two sons and their descendants was given an equal inheritance and considered an equal tribe with the others. Therefore, there were really 13 tribes when the Israelites left Egypt.

The Levites and the Tithe

The Levites were one of the tribes of the nation Israel. Their primary responsibility was to take care of the tabernacle and other spiritual ministries of Israel. They were like the full-time Christian workers of their day and not unlike full time pastors, missionaries, teachers in Bible colleges and seminaries and other Christian workers today. The Levites did not receive an inheritance of land with the other 12 tribes. Though they could plant their own personal gardens they could not compete in the economic market with other Israelites. They were to devote all of their energies to spiritual ministries. The Levites were largely supported by the tithe of the other tribes.

The Old Testament tithe could be used for three general purposes in Israel. Some of it could be used for the various ceremonial meals that the Jews were required to eat (Deuteronomy 12:17-18; 14:22-26). Some of it could be used to give to needy people (Deuteronomy 26:12). However, the bulk of it went to support of the Levites (Numbers 18:21, 24-26; Deuteronomy 14:27; Nehemiah 10:37-38; 12:44; 13:5). An important thing to remember is that the tithe in the Old Testament was always food. It could be monetized so one could go to a distant place and repurchase the necessary food items for sacred meals (Deuteronomy 14:22-26). Therefore, the tithe was always used for people and not projects or buildings.

I believe the 13 tribes of Israel provide us an example of how the church today can take care of her full time Christian workers. Note the pattern: Each of the tribes was required to give ten percent of their income to the Lord to be used for people-related ministries. If each tribe gave ten percent, including the Levites, that would be 130 percent of the average income of each tribe because 13 tribes would be giving it. If it took 30 percent to take care of the needy and the ceremonial meals and other miscellaneous needs, that would leave 100 percent for the Levites. If the Levites received 100 percent of the income the other tribes received, that would allow them to live on the same socio-economic level that their brothers did. They would not live above them so that they might become proud and could not identify with them. They would not live below them so that they would have to worry about financial pressure. Everyone would live on about the same basis.

Modern Levites and the Tithe

How does this pattern apply to us today?

It should influence our building programs.

Building projects in the Old Testament were always built with special offerings not the tithes of God's people. Nowhere in the New Testament did God tell anyone to build buildings. Certainly our church buildings are useful and helpful and make our worship and ministry easier. However, since they are not mentioned in the New Testament, they are not absolutely essential for our Christian work.

A Pastor's Thanksgiving After the Jos Crisis

During the Jos Crisis of September 2001, the Immanuel Baptist Church was burned. This is one of the closest churches to my house in Jos. Eight days later, my family and I worshipped with this church. This was the first time the church had met since the crisis started. The church met at a community hall about one kilometer from the site of the burned out church building. One of the things that impressed me the most was when the pastor said, "I am happy that they were not able to burn our church. Since none of our church members were killed, that means that the church was not burned."

The Old Testament pattern of tithing and giving suggests that buildings should be built with special offerings not tithes. That pattern suggests that buildings should not be maintained with the tithe. Remember, the tithe was always used for people and not projects.

It should influence the church's attitude toward full-time Christian workers.

The model of the 13 tribes suggests to us that wherever there are 13 families, that should be sufficient resources to enable one family to serve the Lord in a full-time capacity. This is conditioned upon the church giving all the tithes to the people and not using them for other things. This practice would enable the full-time family to live on the same socio-economic basis as the other families of the church. If there were 26 families, the church could afford to have two families ministering on a full time basis. Other options would be supporting a missionary family full time or supporting a teacher in a Bible college or seminary.

If our churches would be willing to commit our resources to God's causes in the same way Old Testament saints did—if we would commit ourselves to using tithes for people-related projects and special offerings for all other projects, there would be no lack of support for God's people.

We often think we New Testament believers are better or stronger than our Old Testament brothers because we have much greater knowledge and we have access to the Holy Spirit. In fact, the writer to the Hebrews tells us that God has reserved something *"better"* for us than even for the great heroes of the faith (Hebrews 11:40). However, in terms of commitment of financial resources to God's work, we have a lot to learn from them.

I personally believe that the backbone financial support for any missionary project should be the local church from which the missionary comes.

> *While they [the church leaders] were worshiping the Lord and fasting, the Holy Spirit said, "Set apart for me Barnabas and Saul for the work to which I have called them." So after they had fasted and prayed, they placed their hands on them and sent them off.*
> —(Acts 13:2)

God had spoken to a local church congregation about the first missionary journey. The church at Antioch *"sent them off."* The "sending them off" implies more than just saying "Good-bye. God bless you. We will pray for you." It implies they assumed financial responsibility for the missionary team. It cost money for them to sail from Antioch to the island of Cypress. It cost money to eat along the way. Who paid for it? Though we are not told specifically, I think that it was the church at Antioch because they were the ones who sent them out.

Many churches pride themselves in supporting 50 or even 100 missionaries. However, they are only giving a small portion of the needed budget of each of those missionaries. A better strategy is for a church to take on a larger portion of a fewer number of missionaries' support. It is better for one church to underwrite the expenses of a missionary than for 25 churches to do so.

In light of these observations, I will challenge all local churches with several things:

I challenge every local church to guarantee the full budget of any member who volunteers to go to the mission field. If God chooses to bless a particular church by calling people out of it for his service, this part of the body of Christ should be responsible to meet their needs.

Although I work for the university, I also work for an organization that helps to underwrite our expenses while we serve in Nigeria. Our home church is now underwriting a significant portion of those expenses. That is a great blessing. It enables me to spend a lot of time with that church when I am in the US. In addition, it keeps me from moving around all over the country trying to visit and report to other churches who have given to our ministry. And it frees those other churches to devote their support to other international projects.

I challenge every local church to significantly increase the percentage of your budget you are giving to missions. I briefly attended a church in Columbia, South Carolina, USA in 1973 which had only recently been organized. The pastor was very missions-minded. I spoke in his beautiful church recently. He told me that now, over 50 percent of all money that comes into the church goes to missions. That in my opinion is the way a church should finance missionary work. I think it has been proven many times over that the church that gives to missions will be blessed by God.

I challenge every individual believer to commit more of your personal resources to missionaries and missionary projects. During a recent trip to the US, I visited one of the board members of our organization. He has a large factory with over a hundred employees. He has a nice house but it is not opulent. He drives a 15-year-old vehicle. He enjoys making big money so that he can give most of it away. He is a good model for those who get more money than they need for their own personal needs. He is a great supporter and encourager of missions and missionaries.

Remember Jesus said:

> *Give, and it will be given to you. A good measure, pressed down, shaken together and running over, will be poured into your lap. For with the measure you use, it will be measured to you.*
>
> —Luke 6:38

There are many other things the local church can do for missions. However, one of the most practical and most obvious is to be significantly involved in financing mission projects.

What is God saying to you about financially supporting missions?

Summary

Not everyone can go to the mission field. Some have to stay back and take care of the home base. However, the Philippians demonstrate that home churches can and should pray for their missionaries. They also demonstrate that they should be involved in recruiting more missionaries. And they certainly demonstrate that they should be providing financial support for missionaries. The Philippian Church is a great model and challenge to all churches about how to support missionaries.

CHAPTER 4

SUFFERING

(1:12-14)[1]

Now I want you to know, brothers, that what has happened to me has really served to advance the gospel. As a result, it has become clear throughout the whole palace guard and to everyone else that I am in chains for Christ. Because of my chains, most of the brothers in the Lord have been encouraged to speak the word of God more courageously and fearlessly.

—Phil.1:12-14

In 1:12-17 Paul used some rather sober but significant language to describe his condition:

- "what has happened to me"
- "I am in chains"
- "because of my chains"
- "stir up trouble for me"
- "while I am in chains"

---

[1] One will observe that in the first section, I treated material that includes 1:12-14. However, I was looking at another theme in that section. Because the passage was not exhaustively treated in the first chapter, I have come back to this passage to examine another major theme.

These statements tell us that being a follower of Jesus will not always be easy.

As a teacher and preacher of the Bible for the last 35 years, I have been asked thousands of questions about God, the Bible, Christian theology and related issues. However, there is one question that is asked more than any other. It comes in many different forms and contexts. Sometimes it is asked in an academic manner by a student or seminar participant and at other times it is asked with great passion by someone who is undergoing some kind of suffering or stress. It is this question: *How can a good God who is capable of doing all things, allow good people to suffer?* The assumption is that if God is a good God, and if God is all-powerful, capable of doing anything, that God would relieve the suffering of at least the good people who are trying to serve him.

Most, if not all Christians, struggle with this question. The way you attempt to answer it affects your theology and the focus of your ministry. Many modern Christian leaders have an almost exclusive focus on the positive benefits of Christian faith, to the point of ignoring or even denying the problems Christians may face. They tend to focus on financial and material prosperity as well as physical health.

The Bible does indeed talk about prosperity. One of the first scriptures that many of us memorized was Psalm 1 which describes the blessed man in this way: *"He is like a tree planted by streams of water, which yields its fruit in season and whose leaf does not wither. Whatever he does prospers"* (1:3). However the prosperity referred to is a much more holistic type of prosperity than we normally hear from our modern preachers. It refers to

- the prosperity of a healthy body
- the prosperity of balanced emotions
- the prosperity of good human relationships
- the prosperity of a clean and safe environment

- the prosperity of a meaningful relationship with God
- the prosperity of opportunities for success
- the prosperity of a well-developed mind
- the prosperity of adequate resources
- the prosperity of good governance

Of course, Jesus was concerned about the physical bodies of individuals. He healed the sick. He cast out demons. He even raised the dead. And he gave authority to his disciples to do the same things that he did.

However, this is not the whole story. There are no promises in the Bible that every follower of Jesus will be wealthy nor is there any guarantee that every follower of Jesus will be healthy. It just so happens that 100 per cent of the followers of Jesus throughout the first 20 centuries of Christianity have died. People usually do not die unless there is some kind of sickness or injury. And people usually do not have sickness or injury without suffering. It is the suffering that eventually leads to death. This is the normal pattern of life and Christians are not exempt from it.

The point I want to stress here and the point that Paul illustrates is that suffering is a normal part of the life of every human being, including the followers of Jesus. Eliphaz said, *"Man is born to trouble as surely as sparks fly upward"* (Job 5:7). Whether we like it or not, suffering is a real part of life.

If suffering is a regular part of our lives, then apparently it is not there by accident. There are things that we can learn from it. There are benefits that we can receive from it. Why then does God allow his people to suffer?

Suffering helps to advance the gospel.

"Now I want you to know, brothers, that what has happened to me has really served to advance the gospel" (1:12). At this time, Paul was under house arrest. It appears he was being guarded by soldiers who would be chained to him in three-hour shifts. It is possible that he was being guarded by the elite Palace Guard. Paul was apparently allowed to have visitors. Many came to him and while they were there Paul witnessed to them. Every time Paul told the story of Jesus, in addition to the visitor hearing the story, the soldier chained to him also heard the story. It is likely that many of these soldiers became believers while being chained to Paul; thus, Paul's imprisonment aided in the spread of the gospel.

Chuck Colson's Experience

Many ministries are born in suffering. Chuck Colson was a very close assistant to the president of the United States. However, due to his involvement in the Watergate scandal, he eventually went to prison. Fortunately, shortly before going to prison, he became "born again" according to his own testimony. God used the time in prison to really teach him some important lessons and to prepare him for an important ministry. After he got out of prison, he felt God calling him to create a prison ministry which has now become the largest prison ministry in the world. However, that ministry would not have happened without Chuck Colson having spent time in prison as a convicted felon. His imprisonment helped to advance the gospel.

Some ministries can only be successfully executed in suffering and sacrifice. How can a person minister to drug addicts without sharing in some of their suffering and privation? Is it little wonder that God often calls converted drug addicts and drunkards to go back and work with those same kinds of people?

One of the ministries God started developing in the church in Nigeria and other parts of Africa in the latter part of the twentieth century was a ministry to people living with HIV/AIDS and to their families. How can one minister in those situations without sharing in the suffering of these people? The question is this: Are you willing to suffer to advance the cause of Christ? All of the Christians who have been successful in ministering to the weak and needy in society have interacted with them and shared their pain.

Suffering of Leaders Encourages Believers.

> *Because of my chains, most of the brothers in the Lord have been encouraged to speak the word of God more courageously and fearlessly.*
> —Phil. 1:14

The fact that Paul, the person who led them to faith, was willing to suffer for his faith encouraged the believers to be more bold and fearless in their witness for Christ.

Paul did an amazing thing during his first visit to Philippi. Note these scriptures:

When Paul was in Philippi, he took a beating and chose not reveal the fact that he was a Roman citizen until the next day. However, in Jerusalem, Paul revealed his Roman citizenship before he received the beating and spared himself the beating. The question is why did Paul not reveal his Roman citizenship to the Philippian jailor? We are not told. However, one reason may have been that he was willing to suffer in order to be an encouragement to the new believers in Philippi whom he knew were going to suffer for their faith.

- (Paul in Philippi) *The crowd joined in the attack against Paul and Silas, and the magistrates ordered them to be stripped and* beaten. *After they had been severely flogged, they were thrown into prison, and the jailer was commanded to guard them carefully. Upon receiving such orders, he put them in the inner cell and fastened their feet in the stocks* (Acts 16:22-24).

- (Paul in Jerusalem) *As they were shouting and throwing off their cloaks and flinging dust into the air, the commander ordered Paul to be taken into the barracks. He directed that he be flogged and questioned in order to find out why the people were shouting at him like this. As they stretched him out to flog him, Paul said to the centurion standing there, "Is it legal for you to flog a Roman citizen who hasn't even been found guilty?" When the centurion heard this, he went to the commander and reported it. "What are you going to do?" he asked. "This man is a Roman citizen." The commander went to Paul and asked, "Tell me, are you a Roman citizen?" "Yes, I am," he answered. Then the commander said, "I had to pay a big price for my citizenship." "But I was born a citizen," Paul replied. Those who were about to question him withdrew immediately. The commander himself was alarmed when he realized that he had put Paul, a Roman citizen, in chains* (Acts 22:23-29).

- (Paul in Philippi) *But Paul said to the officers: "They beat us publicly without a trial, even though we are Roman citizens, and threw us into prison. And now do they want to get rid of us quietly? No! Let them come themselves and escort us out"* (Acts 16:37).

Leadership of Alexander the Great

Alexander the Great and his troops were once on a long ten-day march across a desert. On the ninth day, his soldiers had become very tired and weary. They all needed water. Someone brought Alexander a helmet full of water. However, he refused to drink it. He said, "How can I drink water when all my soldiers have no water to drink?" He then poured the water out on the sand. When the soldiers saw this sacrifice on his part, they all shouted and, with renewed energy, they finished the march with great enthusiasm. They had been inspired by the voluntary suffering of their leader.

What is the significance of this for Christian workers and especially for Christian missionaries? Missionaries struggle between two important principles: Identifying with the people and efficiency in their work. If I totally identify with the people that I am serving, I will struggle with the same electrical and water and other infrastructure problems they have and that will seriously affect the efficiency of my ministry. On the other hand, if I focus purely on efficiency, I will create an environment in which I am largely removed from the people that I am serving.

We see negative illustrations of this in the extravagant lifestyles of many of our Christian leaders. With their multiple exotic houses and their sleek jets and their designer clothes, they have little or no comprehension of what the average Christian church member experiences.

Where is the balance of these things? There is no simple formula that gives an automatic answer.

We have to examine our ministries to help determine the answer to that question. If we are doing medical work, we should err on the side of technology. If we are doing evangelism among unreached people groups, perhaps we should err on the side of identifying with the people.

Recently I had a conversation with a respected Nigerian Christian leader about the prosperity gospel. We were discussing where this comes from. He casually mentioned as if everyone knew this: "It comes from the missionaries. They always have vehicles and nice homes. Therefore, as the church grows, we want to be like them."

That was an amazing statement to me. We tend to think that the people will develop our character and accept our beliefs without attempting to imitate our more affluent lifestyles.

What we can say for sure is that when we make a deliberate effort to identify with the people we are serving, there is great appreciation.

- When we do something as simple as wearing local clothes, they appreciate it.
- When we willingly suffer when our friends know that we do not have to, that makes an important point to those we are serving.

Suffering Prepares Believers to Minister to Others.

> *For it has been granted to you on behalf of Christ not only to believe on him, but also to suffer for him, since you are going through the same struggle you saw I had, and now hear that I still have.*
> —Phil. 1:29-30

Paul anticipated that the Philippians were going to suffer. He pointed out that they were going through the same kinds of suffering that he was going through. His courage in the face of trouble surely was a great example to them.

Paul made an interesting statement about suffering in 2 Corinthians 1:3-4,

> *Praise be to the God and Father of our Lord Jesus Christ, the Father of compassion and the God of all comfort, who comforts us in all our troubles, so that we can comfort those in any trouble with the comfort we ourselves have received from God.*

This statement hints at a 6-point argument:

1. The world is filled with hurting people.
2. We are called to help hurting people.
3. God never gives us an assignment without preparing us to do it.
4. The best way to comfort a hurting person is to have been comforted yourself.
5. Unfortunately, the only way to be comforted is to have suffered.
6. Therefore, God allows us to hurt and then be comforted. This prepares us to minister comfort and healing to those who hurt.

Those of us from the western world have insulated ourselves from suffering to a large extent.

- We have medicine to take away our pain.
- We have air-conditioners to take away the heat.
- We have vehicles to take away the stress of trekking.
- We have computers to take away the pain of writing by hand.
- We have TV's, VCR's and DVD's and other devices to take away the boredom of life.
- We have funeral homes to take away the sorrow and stress of dying.

Many ministers and missionaries live above the people they are serving. Therefore, God sometimes allows them to suffer so they can minister to those who are hurting.

Some Christian leaders tell us we are sons of a king; therefore, we should live like a king. However, Jesus said, *"If anyone would come after me, he must deny himself, and take up his cross . . ."* (Matthew 16:24). A cross is an instrument of suffering. What Jesus meant was that Christians must be willing to suffer.

First Question in an African University Classroom

In February 1989, I taught my first class in an African university. At the beginning of the class, I took a little while to introduce the new programme we were starting at the university and also to introduce myself. After I had talked for a while, I gave the students a chance to respond. A middle-aged man in the back of the room asked me this question which was the first question I was ever asked in an African university classroom, "Sir, have you ever suffered?" This student was not interested in what church I belonged to or whether I had a PhD or whether I believed in his particular theology. The thing he was concerned about was whether I had ever suffered. My answer to that question would tell him a lot about the kind of teaching he would be receiving from me.

My dear friends, one of the reasons that you and I have to suffer in this world is because God has called us to work among suffering people. Note these challenging words from 1 Peter 2:21-25:

> *To this you were called, because Christ suffered for you, leaving you an example, that you should follow in his steps. "He committed no sin, and no deceit was found in his mouth."* When they hurled their insults at him, he did not retaliate; when he suffered, he made no threats. Instead, he entrusted himself to him who judges justly. He himself bore our sins in his body on the tree, so that we might die to sins and live for righteousness; by his wounds you have been healed. For you were like sheep going astray, but now you have returned to the Shepherd and Overseer of your souls.

Remember, suffering is not just part of our life; it is part of our ministry.

CHAPTER 5

SELFLESSNESS

(1:15-26)

Somewhere near the heart of Christian living is the principle of selflessness. Paul demonstrates this attitude several different ways in these next few verses and in his other writings.

What is selflessness?

- It is *"in honor, preferring one another."*
- It is *"looking after the welfare of others before yourself."*
- It is *"loving your neighbor as yourself."*
- It is following Jesus' example: He *"loved us and gave himself up for us as a fragrant offering and sacrifice to God."*

I will discuss this in more detail in Philippians 2, but there are two points of application I would like to make at this time.

Paul Was Selfless toward Other Ministries.

> *It is true that some preach Christ out of envy and rivalry, but others out of goodwill. The latter do so in love, knowing that I am put here for the defense of the gospel. The former preach Christ out of selfish ambition, not sincerely, supposing that they can stir up trouble for me while I am in chains. But what does it matter? The important*

> *thing is that in every way, whether from false motives or true, Christ is preached. And because of this I rejoice.*
> —Phil. 1:15-18

Paul acknowledged that some were preaching the gospel of Christ for wrong motives. However, he was gracious toward them and asked that they be allowed to continue preaching. The fact that Christ was being preached was more important than the particular motivation behind that preaching.

Sometimes missionaries and other ministries tend to be territorial. Some years ago, a leader of a large campus ministry came to see me. One of his biggest complaints was the proliferation of campus ministries. He even reported that one Christian organization had written to the vice chancellor of one university asking that there be a suspension of the creation of new Christian campus ministries. Obviously, there may be a time and good reasons to place restrictions on the growth of campus fellowships and ministries. However, I sensed in this complaint more of a territorial spirit than a genuine concern for orderly campus ministry.

We do not own the church or any part of it. God has not given me the franchise for doing university work. It all belongs to Him.

There are limitations of this principle. Paul was not concerned about motives but he was concerned about truth. In 3:2, Paul warned the Philippians against the Judaizers. They were preaching another gospel--not just preaching the true gospel with wrong motives. Therefore, they needed to be opposed.

The point is that there should be no jealousy in ministry. There should be active cooperation with all those who are promoting Jesus Christ.

Let us remember that there are many different members of the body of Christ. Most have different personalities; many even have important differences in theology. However, all of them are doing the work of God. We should encourage one another, not be in competition with one another.

One of the things that I am most grateful to God for is the opportunity to work with the whole body of Christ. Like most Christians, I was reared in a part of the body of Christ that had its own beliefs, its own traditions and its own philosophy of right and wrong. We were a conservative group of believers who were suspicious of anyone who did not believe like we did or who practiced a lifestyle different from our own. However, early in my career I began to see that the body of Christ was much broader than our little group. When I came to Africa and started working in a public university, I had access more than ever to the broader Christian body. I have found that interacting with Christians from different traditions to be a very rewarding experience.

Just as there are different Christians who have different gifts and therefore make different contributions to the body of Christ, in recent years I have begun to see there are different denominations and different movements within Christendom that emphasize different things. And nearly all of these emphases are important. The truth is in the whole body and we need each other to provide balance. Therefore, when some person or group emphasizes beliefs or practices or emphasizes something different than our beliefs, we should not be threatened. Like Paul, we should rejoice that Christ is being preached.

What does this mean for us?

1. We should encourage those doing other ministries.
We should encourage them even if they are not part of us. We should encourage them, even if they believe a little different than we do. We should encourage them even if they have different styles of worship than we do. If they are preaching Christ and attempting to live like

Christ, we should extend to them not only the right hand of fellowship but the warm embrace of encouragement.

2. We should cooperate with those doing other ministries.
I am not a missiologist. I know most of what I know about missions from observation. However, one key thing I see in modern missions is a much greater spirit of cooperation and partnership. The Danish Lutherans have seconded some of their personnel to SIM. The Christian Reformed World Missions (CRC) allows some of its personnel to work with IICS. I am not sure that this was done as much in the past. However, this is exactly the kind of cooperation and selfless kind of ministries that we should be seeing in our missions.

Some years ago, I was working on funding for a Christian Religious Knowledge (CRK) teacher's manual. This is project for the whole body of Christ in Nigeria. I wrote a letter to the CRC missions' director. I was amazed when this mission gave us $10,000 for this project. Another mission gave us $40,000. Another one gave close to $30,000. We eventually received over $80,000 from various foreign mission agencies in Nigeria to do that project. This is the spirit of cooperation and selflessness I believe is characteristic of modern missions. And I pray this will increase and expand.

Paul Was Selfless toward His Body

> *I eagerly expect and hope that I will in no way be ashamed, but will have sufficient courage so that now as always Christ will be exalted in my body, whether by life or by death. For to me, to live is Christ and to die is gain. If I am to go on living in the body, this will mean fruitful labor for me. Yet what shall I choose? I do not know! I am torn between the two: I desire to depart and be with Christ, which is better by far; but it is more necessary for you that I remain in the body.*
> —Phil. 1:20-24

Paul was willing to live or die—whatever God willed. If God wanted him to go, that was fine. If God wanted him to stay, that was fine. He was totally submissive to the will of God in the matter of life and death. This means he was totally selfless. His whole ambition in life was that Christ would be exalted in his life. The total focus of his life was on Christ and not on himself. He was selfless and not self-centered. If Christ could be exalted better through his dying than living, he was content to die.

There are at least two ways we can go to Hillcrest School in Jos from our house. When I got to the junction I would frequently ask our children, "Which way do you want to go?" It really did not matter to me at that point. That is the attitude Paul had with regards to his dying or living.

Maslow's Hierarchy is a pyramid of human values. The most fundamental and basic of all these human values is life. We will protect our life at any expense. And yet God's work requires risks.

Missionary life has its risks. In the 21 years I have lived in Nigeria, I have known of 18 missionaries or missionary children who have died while in Nigeria. A missionary has a greater likelihood of dying in Nigeria than an American soldier had of dying in the first Gulf War.

Should that cause us to stay away from missions? No, we can die anywhere. However, it should make us aware that there are risks involved in mission work.

Selflessness is relaxing in the will of God. It is putting God's will ahead of our own will. It is putting the benefit of others ahead of our own interests. It is promoting Christ and demoting self. It is saying like John the Baptist, *"He must become greater; I must become less"* (John 3:30).

It is one thing to be selfless about other ministries. However, it is a different thing when the pain starts wracking our bodies. Are we willing to suffer some kind of physical handicap in order that the gospel might be promoted? Are we willing to run the risk of imprisonment in order to promote the cause of Christ?

Jesus said, *"Greater love has no one than this, that he lay down his life for his friends"* (John 15:13). Jesus not only spoke those words, he practiced them. He lived a life of selfless sacrifice. Are you willing to follow Christ in his selflessness?

CHAPTER 6

HONORABLE CONDUCT

(1:27-30)

Whatever happens, conduct yourselves in a manner worthy of the gospel of Christ. Then, whether I come and see you or only hear about you in my absence, I will know that you stand firm in one spirit, contending as one man for the faith of the gospel without being frightened in any way by those who oppose you. This is a sign to them that they will be destroyed, but that you will be saved—and that by God. For it has been granted to you on behalf of Christ not only to believe on him, but also to suffer for him, since you are going through the same struggle you saw I had, and now hear that I still have.

—Phil. 1:27-30

One of the realities of being a Christian in the first century Roman world was serious opposition that sometimes led to suffering. Paul had personally experienced such opposition when he first went to Philippi. Once he heard that the Philippian believers were passing through various forms of persecution, he immediately wrote to encourage them to always maintain honorable conduct in the face of their opposition. He described this in several ways.

Determination in the Face of Uncertainty

> *"whatever happens . . . contending for the faith"*
> —Phil. 1:27

The church in Philippi was born in persecution. On his first trip there, Paul was arrested and thrown into prison. However, this did not discourage him. He continued to re-visit Philippi, in spite of the opposition and danger. In fact, he developed a warm relationship with the Philippians, and the Philippian church became one of Paul's big success stories.

Paul was calling the Philippians to this same kind of determination. He told them that whatever happened—whatever obstacles they faced and whatever opposition they encountered, they should continue to contend for the faith. This was not just a call for them to maintain their faith and resist temptation. This was a call for them to continue to publicly proclaim the faith.

I once heard a story about a sergeant leading a small group of soldiers in battle. At one point, he called on the radio, reporting that his platoon was totally surrounded by the enemy. The captain radioed back, asking for his plans. The sergeant replied, "Don't worry, sir. We won't let a one of them escape." That is the kind of attitude that Paul was calling for. Even in the face of the greatest opposition, Paul challenged the Christians to continue making progress.

Two of the songs that my church used to sing were "Hold the Fort" and "Onward Christian Soldiers." I like the second but I am afraid we often live out the first. God is calling us not just to live a defensive life and survive. He is calling us to continue contending for the faith and promoting the faith, even in the face of severe opposition.

Unity in the Face of Conflict

> *"in one spirit . . . as one man"*
>
> —Phil. 1:27b

Paul told the Philippians how they were to contend for the faith. They were to do it *"in one spirit . . . as one man."* Unity is a major theme in Philippians 2. However, at this place I want to stress unity as one faces opposition.

The body of Christ is a diverse body. The hand is not like the ear and the nose is not like the eye. Each part of the body of Christ has a different function and views life from a slightly different perspective. Therefore, having occasional disagreements in the body of Christ is normal, expected and inevitable. However, when the church is being attacked or when individual Christians are being attacked, that is not the time to stress our diversity. That is the time to come together.

In September 2001, Jos experienced a severe ethnic and religious conflict. Because fighting was going on around the university, the university gates were locked with 4000 students and staff inside. They stayed there all night. Some boys attempted to scale the university wall to attack those inside. All those inside banded together to resist the attackers. Tribe was not important; religion was not an issue; gender did not matter. All the students and staff, Christians and Muslims, undergraduate and postgraduate, men and women, worked together to protect themselves. The issue was there was an enemy outside who wanted to harm people inside.

That is the point I think Paul is making here. Though there were believers with different points of view in the Philippian church, whenever the church was being attacked, there had to be unity. That is just as true today as it was 2000 years ago.

- If some Christians are restricted in practicing or promoting their faith, all Christian believers must stand together.
- If government attempts to remove the teaching of religious instruction from our public schools, all Christians must stand together.
- If Christians are refused permission to build church buildings because of illegal and unfair reasons, Christians must stand together.

Perhaps the biggest attack on the church today is the HIV/AIDS crisis. This enemy does not care what church people attend or what denomination they belong to. It is an enemy that has come to kill and steal and destroy (John 10:10). Therefore, we Christians must take a very united stand against this enemy. That means we must share resources and share ideas. That means we should hold joint training workshops. That means that we must be one in spirit and fight this enemy as one person.

Courage in the Face of Opposition

"without being frightened in any way by those who oppose you"
—Phil. 1:28

Fear is perhaps the biggest obstacle we face during times of opposition. Fear is natural. Fear is built into our human psychological nature to help us survive. Fear of the water keeps people from drowning. Fear of snakes makes people cautious when they are in the bush. Fear of high places keeps people from getting into dangerous places.

However, like all good things, fear can be perverted. Fear can keep us from doing good and righteous deeds. Fear of what unbelievers will think about us can keep us from doing the right thing. Fear of talking to strangers can keep us from witnessing for Christ. Fear of public speaking can keep us from getting involved in public ministries of the church. Fear of violence and persecution can neutralize a Christian and can even cause some people to run away from their Christian faith.

However, Paul was calling the Philippian believers to be courageous—to overcome the natural fear they have of people who oppose them. And Paul was able to do this from a remarkable position of strength. As we have seen earlier, Paul was able to encourage people to overcome their fear because he had done exactly that in Philippi. He had taken a beating even though he was a Roman citizen and was exempt from such things. Perhaps this is what he had in mind when he wrote a verse or two later *"since you are going through the same struggle you saw I had and now hear that I still have"* (1:30).

Most Christians face little opposition in their Christian walk. However, when we do face opposition, whether from family, clan, colleagues in our work place, people from other religions or any other kind of opposition, Paul is calling us to be courageous. The Apostle John, who lived longer than any of the other apostles and therefore had more opportunities than any of the others to face opposition, wrote, *"There is no fear in love. But perfect love drives out fear . . ."* (1 John 4:18).

Faith in the Face of Suffering

> *"For it has been granted to you on behalf of Christ not only to believe on him, but also to suffer for him"*
> —Phil. 1:29

Faith is believing the truth and doing the right thing even when we do not understand. There are many things we do not understand in this world. However, one of the most difficult things to understand is why God allows innocent people to suffer.

This is a question even some people in the Bible asked. Asaph, author of Psalm 73, could not understand why the wicked seemed to prosper, while he, a minister of music in the Temple, seemed to suffer so much. Habbakuk, a prophet of God, could not understand why God would allow wicked people to go unpunished for so long. When God did tell him that he was raising up the Chaldeans to punish the Israelites, Habbakuk could not understand why God could use people who were more wicked to punish those who were less wicked. It is indeed difficult to understand and explain these things.

However, faith is believing and doing the right thing even when we do not understand. Job could not understand why he was suffering. He raised all kinds of questions and came close to accusing God of wrong doing. However, in the end, he continued to keep his faith in God and continued to do the right thing, even though he did not understand. And, when his testing time was over, God held him up as an outstanding example of faith and obedience.

Paul knew that the Philippians were going to suffer. He could not anticipate every question that the Philippians might raise during their times of suffering and he probably could not have answered all those questions even if he knew the questions. However, he called on the Philippians to continue believing in Christ, even in times of suffering.

CHAPTER 7

UNITY

(2:1-3)

If you have any encouragement from being united with Christ, if any comfort from his love, if any fellowship with the Spirit, if any tenderness and compassion, then make my joy complete by being like-minded, having the same love, being one in spirit and purpose.
—Phil. 2:1-2

In this section, Paul was encouraging the Philippians to *"make my joy complete."* The book of Philippians is a book about joy. Many commentators include joy as the theme of the book in one way or another. This is remarkable in light of the fact that Paul was a prisoner when he wrote it. You would think that a letter from prison would be filled with whining and complaining, but it is not. It is filled with examples and exhortations about joy.

How could Paul's joy be made complete? He partially answered this question in 2:2, *"then make my joy complete by being like minded, having the same love, being one in spirit and purpose."* In the previous verse, Paul had written, *"If you have any encouragement from being united with Christ . . ."* Paul was stating that if the Philippians wanted to make him happy, if they wanted him to be filled with joy, they needed to have a spirit of unity.

Joy in ministry is inseparably linked with unity in ministry. What is joy? It is difficult to define. Joy is a more long-lasting good feeling than other good feelings. It is a feeling of peace, satisfaction and fulfillment that creates positive emotions.

It is easier to illustrate joy than define it. Here is a fine young man waiting for a beautiful young lady at the altar, in the process of being married. That is a picture of joy. Here is a fine young man looking over the shoulder of his wife who has recently given birth to their first child. That is a picture of real joy.

A good way to try to understand a particular truth is to look at its opposite. What would be the opposite of joy? The first thing that comes to my mind is sadness or grief. Here is a young couple looking into the face of their son lying in a coffin. That is grief and that is the opposite of joy.

For me, one of the most severe forms of grief is disunity, the failure to be likeminded, not having the same love and not being one in spirit and purpose. I am a "people person" and perhaps these things affect me differently than others. One thing that steals my joy quicker than anything else is when a misunderstanding or conflict or some other barrier comes between another person and me.

The point is simple: Being united in spirit is a source of great joy. Being divided in spirit and purpose is a great source of grief and stress.

Successful people, by their nature, are strong opinionated people; they are leaders; they are independent thinkers. They always have opinions about things. Therefore, it would not be surprising to find within a successful church or successful business or successful family some rather strong disagreements about policies, projects, personnel and other things.

We are all members of one body and that body is made up of members with different functions. Naturally the hand would have a difference of opinion about eating than the tongue. The nose thinks that the only thing that is important is smelling but although the ear is only a few inches away, it is convinced that hearing is far more important than smelling.

What is the secret of being united? It is being united in the way Paul suggested in this passage.

We Must Be United in Mind

Philippians 2:2 records these words, *"being like-minded."* This word literally means "that you might think the same things." It is not normal, healthy or even possible for us all to think exactly the same thoughts. I think the point Paul is making could be better understood in the modern idiom: "be on the same wave length."

We do not understand why a person would get in an airplane, hijack it and fly it into a building, killing himself and many other innocent people. Most people do not understand that kind of thinking. However, many people cannot understand why a father who is struggling to get enough food to eat, will take ten percent of his income and give it to the church. People cannot understand why a man with a promising career like a businessman or engineer would give up all of that in order to go into the ministry or even to the mission field. However, those on the same "wave length" understand those things perfectly.

When my children have gone back to the US, I have found it interesting that they continued their relationships with their friends from Nigeria. Few young people in North America can really understand them. They do not know what they have experienced nor how they think. However, their friends who were raised in the same place and went to the same school and shared the same experiences continue to be their friends even long after their college careers are over because they are on the same wave length.

Actually the more common experiences persons share, the more they will think alike. Although we Christians come from many different ethnic backgrounds, different church backgrounds, different socio-economic backgrounds and even different countries, we share so many things in common because we are part of the same body of Christ.

Meeting a "Brother" in Port Harcourt

When we first moved to Port Harcourt, one day I met an oil worker from my home state, Louisiana. We spoke the same language; we ate the same food; we were really "brothers." My wife and I invited him to our house for a special American meal. We talked and laughed and told jokes from our area. We had a very enjoyable visit. Later, we invited him for a second meal. However, this time, we found that we had less to talk about and the visit was a bit more strained. After the second visit, it became obvious to us that just because we were from the same state did not mean that we were on the same wavelength. This man was not a believer. He was not interested in church or missions or theological education or other things that I was interested in. Therefore, we really had very little in common and, because of that, our relationship soon lapsed for lack of common interest.

I learned one very interesting thing from that experience. I felt much more comfortable around people who are from a different race, who speak a different language, and who obviously come from a different culture, but were fellow believers, than I did with a man who came from my same place. We have a proverb in my country that says "blood is thicker than water," meaning that we will always feel closer to those who are our relatives. However, the cross is thicker than blood. Those who are fellow believers are our real brothers and sisters.

Paul declared that we Christians must be united in the way we think.

We Must Be United in Love.

Paul wrote, *"having the same love"* (2:2c). What does it mean to have the same love? It means that we have the same kind of love. Our love is selfless love, which means we put others first in our lives. The natural man has a natural love for his family and close friends. That is reflected by the Greek word *philos*. The depraved man has a sensual love that corrupts the God-given sexual love. This is reflected by the Greek word *eros*. The godly man or woman has a divine love that does good to everyone regardless of how lovable that person might be or whether he or she reciprocates that love. This is reflected by the Greek word *agape*.

Agape love is the love that gives. Agape love is the love of the will not the emotions. It chooses to treat another person lovingly regardless of how one feels about that person. This is the only kind of love that you can exercise toward your enemies. Your enemies are the people who mistreat and abuse you. It is difficult to develop a feeling of warm affection towards those people like the feeling you have toward your family. However, you can make a decision to treat those persons lovingly.

We love the same objects. We love God first and foremost. We love our fellow Christians. We even love our enemies. Jesus said; *"By this all men will know that you are my disciples, if you love one another"* (John 13:35). We may not always think alike, but the differences in the way we think should not interfere with our love for one another.

We Must Be United In Soul

The word translated *"one in spirit"* (2:2d) is the Greek *sumpsuchoi* which literally means "with the soul." To be united in soul is a much deeper bond than just being united in mind. Two men may intellectually agree but not like each other. On the other hand, two people may strongly disagree on some topics but have a very warm personal relationship with one another.

Wesley and Whitfield

John Wesley and George Whitefield seriously disagreed theologically. John Wesley was Arminian in his theology while George Whitefield was Calvinistic. In fact Wesley once told Whitefield that if he ever preached his strong brand of Calvinism in one of Wesley's meetings again, he would never let him preach again. Whitefield went straight to the pulpit and preached his beliefs as strongly as he possibly could. However, Wesley and Whitefield continued to be the best of friends. After Whitefield died, someone, knowing their strong disagreements, asked Wesley if he thought he would see Whitefield in heaven. Wesley replied, "No." The bystanders were shocked and thought they had discovered a wonderful piece of gossip until Wesley added, "I expect that George Whitfield will be so much closer to God's throne than I am that I will never be able to see him." Wesley and Whitefield were not always one in mind but they were one in soul.

It is my prayer that you will be united in soul—that you will be true soul brothers and sisters.

We Must Be United in Purpose.

Finally, Paul wrote, *"one . . . in purpose"* (2:2e). The phrase uses the same word referred to above which deals with the mind. It means something like *"minding one thing."* However, most interpreters believe it has to do with having a common purpose or goal.

Our world is filled with much disunity.

- *Disunity from Tribalism.* One ethnic group or one part of the nation tries to dominate another. The person on the top seat only gives jobs or opportunities to people of his or her area.
- *Disunity from Sexism.* Women want more rights; men want to keep women in their place. This creates enmity between men and women.
- *Disunity from Class-ism.* The poor and working class resent the wealthy and believe they are getting an oversized share of the national cake. The elites view the poor as uneducated and incapable of making responsible decisions.
- *Disunity from Generationalism.* The young people resent the old. The old misunderstand the young. Both see things from their own viewpoint.
- *Disunity from Politics-ism.* Different groups believe government should be run differently and cannot unite to solve these problems.
- *Disunity from Religious Conviction.* Christians and Muslims view the other religion with suspicion and are convinced that their group is not being treated fairly.
- *Disunity from Personal Conflict.* People tend to have strong opinions about things and often separate from and criticize others because of personal differences.

However, the disunity that Paul was concerned about was the disunity in the church. Paul wanted the followers of Jesus to be united in purpose. What are the purposes that Christians have in common?

The Christian's overall purpose is to honor Jesus. A personal goal is to come to the measure of the stature of Christ—to be fully conformed to the image of Jesus. The evangelistic goal is to win as many people to Christ as possible. The ministry goal is to fulfill the calling and use the gifts that God has given us. I believe that it is God's will that we be united in these things.

Let us recognize that we will have differences of opinion on doctrines and methods but let us concentrate on those areas where we have serious agreements so we can experience the joy of unity. Specifically, let us focus on Christ whom we all accept as Lord and Savior.

When Jesus created the strategy for spreading the gospel around the world, he created a team approach. He selected 12 people who would begin the process. In order for us to succeed in doing God's work, we are going to have to develop a team spirit. That means that cooperating together to do God's work is one of the most important parts of the Christian faith.

If this is true, then that means that destroying the spirit of unity and cooperation will be one of the most important weapons of the devil. We see those kinds of attacks being made on the body of Christ in the New Testament.

- Satan tried to create disunity in Acts 6 between Greek-speaking and Aramaic speaking widows.
- Satan tried to create disunity in the early church over the Gentiles coming into the church.
- Satan tried to create disunity between Paul and Barnabas over the issue of whether to take Mark on the second missionary journey.
- Satan tried to create disunity between Paul and Peter over Peter's refusal to eat with Gentiles in Antioch.
- Satan tried to create disunity in the Philippian church so that Paul was forced to try to solve the conflict between Euodia and Syntyche.
- Satan tried to create disunity in the Corinthian church by encouraging different factions over who should be the leader of the church.

Satan recognizes that one of the biggest threats to his kingdom is a unified body of Christ. Therefore, he is doing everything possible to try to interrupt that unity and cooperation.

A Conflict in Church over Race

I have had several rather traumatic experiences in my life. Perhaps the one that was the most severe was the time when we had a serious conflict in the church over race. Between 1980 and 1986 I served as the pastor of a church in a rural community in southern Georgia. Unfortunately, some of the older church members tended to have racist attitudes.

On one occasion I aided an African American church and publicly identified with them during one of their special celebrations commemorating the gains they had made. Some of the older members of my church became angry. They felt that I had disgraced our church by my attempts at "mixing the races" and demanded I resign. According to them, I had destroyed my reputation and could no longer serve the white community.

This experience created great shock and grief. Although this was a minority opinion in the church, it greatly affected me. It destroyed my motivation. It robbed me of the joy in doing God's work. It encouraged me to look for ministries elsewhere. It discouraged me from wanting to build up that church, if some of its leaders were going to have such racist attitudes. It created a sense of distrust and suspicion and confusion in our church that took a very long time to overcome. I am grateful to the Lord for helping us to work our way through this issue. Eventually the church and I both recovered from that devastating experience. However, I would guess there was a six month period in my church when nothing significant happened. We continued to meet and worship and pray and do all the other things that churches do.

Unfortunately, our worship and ministries were reduced to just the routine because of the debilitating influence of disunity.

Perhaps the biggest danger our churches will face is internal disagreements that degenerate into division and disunity. The early Christians had disagreements. There were disagreements over what to do with the Gentiles. Paul even had to publicly rebuke Peter over this issue. However, eventually the early missionaries resolved this issue and moved forward with a united front. There were disagreements over personnel. Paul and Barnabas seriously disagreed over what to do with John Mark. They eventually resolved the issue peacefully and moved forward. Fortunately, the early church learned how to overcome those things that sparked disunity and move forward.

Disunity and the Missionary

What are the kinds of disunity that missionaries are likely to experience?

- They may disagree with their mission leaders.
- They may have disagreements with fellow missionaries in the field and even with those at home.
- They may have disagreements with their indigenous church leaders. Often these disagreements arise over cultural issues.

How to Restore Unity

In the first verse in this section, Paul declares that we are *"united in Christ"* (2:1). The ultimate answer to restoring our unity is for us to re-focus on the proper object. If we keep focused on Christ, it is unlikely that we are going to experience fellowship-breaking disunity. When we do experience such things, it means we have probably gotten our focus away from Christ and on some of the other issues related to our religion. Therefore, the answer is to re-focus on Christ.

Jesus himself gives us some practical suggestions about what to do when we experience some break of fellowship with another brother.

> *Therefore, if you are offering your gift at the altar and there remember that you brother has something against you, leave your gift there in front of the altar. First go and be reconciled to your brother; then come and offer your gift.*
>
> —Matthew 5:23-24

Unity is not an automatic thing. It takes effort to maintain that unity and, as Jesus teaches, it takes deliberate effort to restore that unity when it has been lost.

Summary

Psalm 133 states:

> *How good and pleasant it is when brothers live together in unity! It is like precious oil poured on the head, running down on the beard, running down on Aaron's beard, down upon the collar of his robes. It is as if the dew of Hermon were falling on Mount Zion. For there the Lord bestows his blessing, even life forevermore.*

Unity is one of the best things about the Christian faith and, therefore, is one of the first things that the enemy attacks. We must resolve to develop and maintain unity and resist all the enemy's attempts to create division and strife. We must attempt to answer the prayer of Jesus that he prayed on his last night on this earth, that his followers *"may be one as we are one"* (John 17:11). God is a God of unity and he expects that his people will have that same quality.

CHAPTER 8

HUMILITY

(2:3-11)

Definition of Humility (2:3a)

Paul's definition of humility is to *"consider others better than yourselves"* (2:3b). This is a very high standard to achieve. There is a natural instinct within us to protect ourselves and build ourselves up and to promote ourselves. However, Paul wrote that to really be humble, we must consider the other person better than ourselves.

Here in Africa, we believe in giving honor to whom honor is due. That means that we treat big men with respect. It is hard for a big man to be humble in Nigeria. Your briefcase is carried for you. You get the better seats at all functions. You eat first. And you drink Maltinas rather than *kunu*. To be honest, most people, including myself, enjoy the benefits of being treated like a special person.

As long as my son, Daniel, was in Nigeria, whenever we went somewhere together, I had to remind him to carry my briefcase. He would say, "Ah, Dad, we are Americans. In America everyone carries his own briefcase." And I would reply, "But we are in Africa right now and you do not want to be viewed as a disrespectful son." Once, Daniel and I had taken a trip to South Africa and everywhere we went he carried my briefcase. However, we flew from Johannesburg to London and when we got there he said, "Dad, we are out of Africa. I think you can carry your own briefcase now."

When I used to fly from Lagos over to Port Harcourt, when we are boarding, I often watched the big men in their flowing *baban rigas* walk casually from the terminal and go to the front of the line. That has always been very difficult for my American mind to understand. In the USA, there is a much greater stress on equality and human rights. No one goes to the front of the queue in the USA. If some big man tried that in the USA, some 18-year-old strong young man would walk up to him and ask him who he thinks he is and throw him out of the line.

Because older and successful people are treated with respect in Africa, we have to work harder at understanding and practicing humility than in other places.

Application of Humility (2:3b-4)

Negative Side

After giving us a definition or description of humility, Paul then made a very practical application. He wrote, *"Do nothing out of selfish ambition or vain conceit"* (2:3a). This is not really difficult to understand but it is difficult to practice. What was Paul saying? We are to do nothing to make ourselves look better or more important than we really are.

A Proud Young Man in Lagos Airport

One of the first times I came to Nigeria, I was sitting in the Nigerian Airways waiting room at the domestic airport. There were so many things that were new to me. The weather was hot and was only marginally affected by the ceiling fans that were turning slowly above us. I had no idea what the announcer was saying over the PA system. At one point, a man came around clicking a pair of scissors. Although

I had not seen this before, I soon figured out that he was a person who trimmed fingernails and toenails. Finally, he found a customer. A young man who appeared to be about 25 reached out his hands to the fingernail trimmer without saying a word to him or even looking at him. The man trimmed his fingernails. Again, without looking, the young man removed his feet from his shoes and allowed the man to trim his toenails. When the nail trimmer finished his job, the "big" young man reached into his pocket and handed him some money, again without even looking at him. There never was a word exchanged between the two and as far as I could tell the big man never even looked at the small boy. This appeared to be some kind of game. The young man wanted everyone in the waiting room to know that it was beneath his dignity to speak to or even look at the poor fingernail trimmer.

Paul was stating that this is not the attitude that a man of God is to have. He was prohibiting pride in this context. Humility is the opposite of pride.

Positive Side

Paul continued: *"Each of you should look not only to your own interest, but also to the interests of others"* (2:4). This is a very strong statement. The old King James Version actually comes closer to the original meaning. *"Look not every man on his own things, but every man also on the things of others."* The Greek does not have the word "only" in it. It simply says that we are not to look out after our own things but after those of others.

Obviously this is figure of speech. It is a common Hebrew idiom that makes an absolute statement for a relative fact. It is correctly interpreted by the NIV translators. We should not only be interested in our own projects and our own things. We should be interested in and committed to the things of others. This is the high-water mark of humility, being so interested in the success of other people that you actually suffer yourself.

A Selfless Farmer

I had a farmer in my church once named Edwin Pace, who practiced this principle during every harvest season. Edwin had a large tractor-combine and would use that to help his neighbours harvest their crops each year. I noticed that every year he would help get all his neighbours' soybeans harvested before harvesting his own, even though the longer he waited, the more his soybeans would fall on the ground and be lost. Edwin Pace was a selfless farmer.

Illustration of Humility (2:5-11)

> *Your attitude should be the same as that of Christ Jesus: Who, being in very nature God, did not consider equality with God something to be grasped, but made himself nothing, taking the very nature of a servant, being made in human likeness. And being found in appearance as a man, he humbled himself and became obedient to death—even death on a cross!*
>
> —Phil. 2:5-8

If you had to summarize the characteristic of Christ from this paragraph in one word, you would probably select the word humility. Verse 8 says Christ *"being found in appearance as a man, he **humbled himself** . . ."* Christ was completely God in every way. However, he did not view all of the aspects of his divine nature as something that he needed to hold onto, so he freely and voluntarily yielded them up in order to become a man.

The word "humbled" in this context is the word *keneo*, which literally means "emptied." Although the scholars disagree over exactly what is implied by this statement, in some sense of the word, Jesus had to empty himself in order to became human. Why did he have to do that? He had to empty himself because there are some things that are incompatible between God and man.

- God knows all things; human beings must learn things. Was Jesus going to become a man who already knew all things or was he going to be a man who had to learn?
- God is everywhere present; human beings are limited to be at one place at one time. Was Jesus going to continue to utilize the omnipresence quality or was he going to be a real man—limited to being in one place at one time?
- God can do all things; human beings are limited and can do only some things. Was Jesus going to live a supernatural life all throughout his life or was he going to live a normal human life with all of its limitations?

Therefore, if Jesus were really going to identify with humanity and become a human in the fullest sense of the word, he had to yield up some of his divine characteristics.

- In order to learn like a human, Jesus had to empty himself of his divine knowledge.
- In order to learn to walk and talk and read, Jesus had to empty himself of the knowledge of those things to be fully human and experience things as a human.
- In order to experience the same limitations of humans, Jesus had to empty himself of unlimited energy and power and become hungry and tired and sleepy.

Some theologians like to say Jesus did not actually give up those rights but temporarily suspended the use of them.

A Governor Becomes a Traffic Warden

When I was living in Port Harcourt, I once heard a story about one of the military governors going somewhere with his large entourage of vehicles when suddenly they encountered a serious go-slow. After a couple of minutes, the governor got out of his vehicle and started directing traffic until the traffic jam was removed.

As governor, there was no need for this man to start acting like a traffic warden. This was not part of the job description of a military governor. In fact, this was far too small a task for the governor of a state. The governor could have ordered his commissioner of transportation to go out there and solve that problem. However, he temporarily set aside the honor and privilege of being the governor of the state so that he could solve a particular problem. Please note that there was no time when he was directing traffic that he was anything less than the governor of the state. He had not given up his rights as governor. He would have still been addressed as "His Excellency." The governor had simply suspended the free exercise of his rights in order to accomplish a specific job.

We believe Jesus did something like that. He did not give up his right to be God. He was fully and completely God the whole time he was here on this earth. He could still be worshipped and he could still forgive sins. However, in order to fully identify with humanity, he temporarily suspended some of his divine rights and privileges.

The bottom line is the core characteristic that we see in Jesus is humility. That is the primary quality of Christ that we want to see formed in us. However, that humility is manifested in some other interrelated characteristics suggested in this passage. We will briefly examine those now.

Three Key Manifestations of Humility

In this passage we see three interrelated and overlapping characteristics related to humility.

Selflessness

"*Who, being in very nature God, did not consider equality with God something to be grasped . . .*" (2:6). This passage tells us that in his true nature Jesus was God. However, he did not consider equality with God or the fact that he had all of the characteristics and privileges of God something to be held onto. Therefore, he willingly gave up those characteristics or at least the free exercise of those characteristics in order to fulfill the task he came to this earth to do.

The primary moral characteristic I see in this passage is selflessness. The incarnation of Jesus is the ultimate example of selflessness. Think of what Jesus had to give up.

- He had to give up the constant communion with the Trinity.
- He had to give up the loyal adoration and service of angels.
- He had to give up a holy environment of absolute perfection.
- And think of what Jesus had to experience.
- He was born among the animals.
- He was reared and lived in the home of a poor family.
- He had to be misunderstood and abused like any other child.
- He had to go to school and learn to read and write like any other child.
- He had to experience all of the other hardships of that part of the world, including heat and cold and hunger and tiredness and sickness and accidents and injuries and the suffering from losing loved ones.

Jesus voluntarily gave up all of those privileges and accepted all of these liabilities so that he could come to this earth and serve humanity and ultimately provide salvation for us.

Selflessness is giving up our rights to improve the life of someone else. Selflessness is one of the characteristics of Christ that Paul would like to see formed in us. There can never be a greater demonstration of selflessness than we see in the life of Christ.

- Matthew 16:24, *"Then Jesus said to his disciples, 'If anyone would come after me, he must deny himself and take up his cross and follow me.'"*
- Romans 12:10, *"Be devoted to one another in brotherly love. Honor one another above yourselves."* (KJV *"in honor preferring one another."*)
- 1 Corinthians 10:24, *"Nobody should seek his own good, but the good of others."*
- Philippians 2:3-4, *"Do nothing out of selfish ambition or vain conceit, but in humility consider others better than yourselves. Each of you should look not only to your own interests, but also to the interests of others."*

God is calling all of us to a life of selflessness—to a life in which we voluntarily give up our rights in order to bring salvation and other benefits to other people.

Of all the many different kinds of Christian workers, it seems to me the missionary is the kind of Christian who identifies most with Jesus in his selflessness.

- The missionary leaves the fellowship of his family and goes to a foreign country where things are much different than home.
- The missionary often becomes like a little child in the new country and has to learn such basic things as how to talk and communicate.
- The missionary often lives in a situation that is far less comfortable and convenient than the one he left behind.

In other words, to be effective, the missionary has to learn to practice selflessness.

What kind of missionary are you? Are you one who is willing to give up your rights in order to provide salvation and a better life for other people? To what extent are you willing to give up things?

- Are you willing to give up time and regular interaction with your family?
- Are you willing to give up freedom from tropical diseases?
- Are you willing to give up safety and security?
- Are you willing to give up your rights to the privacy you enjoyed before?
- Are you willing to give up the food from your home country?

By volunteering to become a missionary, you have already given up those rights. I congratulate you on that. However, we must continue to remind ourselves that when we got on the airplane, we did indeed give up those rights. Now that we are here and understand this better, are we still willing to voluntarily give up those rights?

In some sense of the word, I respect a missionary more for staying on the mission field than for going to the mission field? Before you came, you did not know what you were getting into. However, now that you are here, you fully understand what it means to be a missionary. The second term missionary is the true missionary, because when he returns to the field the second time he gives up rights knowing what that really means.

Service

"... *but made himself nothing, taking the very nature of a servant, being made in human likeness*" (2:7). This verse stresses another aspect of Jesus' humility.

Paul says that although he was of the nature of God, he took upon himself the nature of a servant. The word "servant" here is the word *doulos* which is the word most often translated slave. To use a term that the teenagers would understand: Jesus morphed from God to being a slave. There is no higher person in the universe than God. There is no one in the human race lower than a slave. Therefore Jesus made the greatest change possible.

The key thought I want to stress here is what a slave does. He serves. So a second important aspect of the nature of Christ is the concept of service. Jesus came to this world not to receive but to serve. He came to this world not to be honored but to serve. He came to this world not to be served but to serve. How did Jesus serve?

- Jesus served his father in the carpenter's shop.
- Jesus served his friends by helping to provide wine for a wedding.
- Jesus served many people by healing their bodies.
- Jesus served at least three families by raising their loved ones from the dead.
- Jesus served the worshippers at the temple by dealing with those who were taking advantage of them.
- Jesus served his disciples by washing their feet.
- Jesus served the whole world by dying on the cross.

One of the major reasons that God created us human beings was to be his servants on this earth. Remember the first words that God ever said to the human race were *"Be fruitful and increase in number; fill the earth and subdue it. Rule over the fish of the sea and the birds of the air and over every living creature that moves on the ground"* (Genesis 1:28). God created the human race to be his workers and take care of the earth. After the human race fell into sin, God had to modify his plan so human beings could take care of fellow human beings. Paul said to the Galatians, *"You, my brothers, were called to be free. But do not use your freedom to indulge the sinful nature; rather, serve one another in love."* (5:13).

In fact, God even measures greatness by the way we serve others. After the incident in which James and John requested the seats on either side of Jesus in his kingdom, Jesus said,

> *You know that those who are regarded as rulers of the Gentiles lord it over them, and their high officials exercise authority over them. Not so with you. Instead, whoever wants to become great among you must be your servant, and whoever wants to be first must be slave of all. For even the Son of Man did not come to be served, but to serve, and to give his life as a ransom for many.*
> —Mark 10:42-45.

Here is the point: When Jesus came to this earth, his nature was changed to be a servant. God created us from the beginning to be servants. Therefore, one of the greatest things we can do is to serve others. If we do not naturally have a servant spirit, God wants to change us into the image of Jesus and form a servant spirit in us.

Missionaries historically have been some of the greatest servants in Christianity. Therefore, the missionary should be by nature a servant. God did not bring you to Nigeria to have people serve you. Fortunately, most of us have people who come to our house and help serve us. However, we must remember that they are helping to serve us so that we can provide a greater service to Nigeria. And even as these people are serving us, we must make sure that we are serving them as well. A slave is a person without any rights. If you focus too much on your rights, you will not be an effective missionary.

What kind of servant missionary are you? Has the servanthood of Jesus been formed in your character?

Sacrifice

"And being found in appearance as a man, he humbled himself and became obedient to death—even death on a cross!" (2:8). In this passage, Paul stresses one of the greatest aspects of Jesus' humility. He humbled himself to the point that he subjected himself to death. And it was not just any death. It was the painful and shameful death on the cross. This suggests to me the word sacrifice. Jesus sacrificed his life on the cross.

What is sacrifice? It is voluntarily giving up something for someone else. Jesus voluntarily gave up his life in order that the world could be saved.

Jesus is not the last person to give up his life for the sake of the gospel. Note that most of the leaders of the church died premature deaths, including the following:

- Stephen
- Eleven of the twelve disciples
- The Apostle Paul

Foreign Missionaries Who Died in Nigeria

Church history is filled with examples of Christians who died for their faith. Even Nigeria has lost a number of expatriate missionaries in Nigeria since I moved to Nigeria in 1988:

- Larry Morrison, a missionary in Akwa Ibom was killed by electrocution.
- Ralph Mason, EYN missionary, was killed in Adamawa in an automobile accident.
- Leon Griffiths, Mission Africa missionary, was killed in Kogi State in automobile accident.

- Hyo Jin Lee, child of Korean missionaries, was killed in Yankari in auto accident.
- Johanna Herrmann, daughter of German missionaries, died in Jos from a tropical disease.
- Justin Ward, five-year old son of SIM missionaries, died in Jos from drowning.
- Bob Wandersee, Lutheran missionary, was killed on the Samanaka Road near Jos by armed robbers.
- Jan Peter Baan, Dutch missionary, was killed in Ebonye State by armed robbers.
- Darrel Foltz, Church of Christ missionary, was killed in Cross River State by armed robbers.
- Cathy Hamlin, a Church of Christ missionary, died in Jos from heart attack.
- Jim Collins, SIM missionary, died near Gombe in a public transportation vehicle accident.
- Ron Boot, short term missionary with the United Missionary Church of Africa, died in Taraba State in mountain climbing accident.

Nigerian Missionaries Who Died in the Line of Duty

It is not only expatriate missionaries who have died in the line of service. Many Nigerians missionaries have also died.

Selzing Swalde, a missionary to the Fulani people group in Taraba State died from an illness that may have been treated in an urban area. Other Nigerian missionaries who have died in similar circumstances include Ezekiel Gigin, Joseph Maroh, Clara Aderonmu, Gloriah Obah, and Esther Kingsley.

Those who have died in automobile accidents while in active missionary service include Gbenga Asthroph, Tolani Omoruyi, Esther Akpo and Brom Sam.

One of the real twenty-first century Nigerian missionary martyrs was Mark Obisike Ojunta. He was a CAPRO (Calvary Ministries, Nigeria's largest indigenous faith mission) project manager who was called to missionary work in 2003. He and his family served among the Kotoko people group in Borno State. He continued to serve in this place even after receiving threats from the radical Islamic sect Boko Haram. Unfortunately, on 27 August 2011, Boko Haram insurgents came to his house and shot him. He died the following day, leaving behind his wife, Ema and two children. Four days earlier, Mark had been contacted about taking a position with CAPRO in the UK. However, he declined because of his commitment to the Kotoko people.

Pastors in Nigeria Who Died in the Line of Duty

It is not only missionaries who die in the field. Nigeria has lost dozens of pastors in northern Nigeria during the last few years due to attacks from Islamic terrorists. The following is a small sample of those pastors who have died in the line of duty.

- Pastor Michael Medugu, a District pastor of the Deeper Life Bible Church, Maiduguri, was killed in his church.
- Reverend Innocent Chukwuemeka Mari, an Assemblies of God pastor, was killed in Southern Kaduna.
- Rev. David Usman, 45, a pastor with the Church of Christ in Nations (COCIN), was killed in Maiduguri.
- Rev. Sabo Yakubu, COCIN Church pastor, was killed in Bauchi by Boko Haram militants.

- Ilaisha Kabura, 70 year old retired COCIN pastor, was killed in his home in Maiduguri.
- Pastor George Orjih, pastor of the Good News of Christ Church International, Inc. and MA seminary student at Jos ECWA Seminary, was beheaded in Maiduguri by militants. Rev. Sabo Yakubu, COCIN pastor and Rev. Sylvester Akpan of National Evangelical Mission were also beheaded in the same incident.
- Rev. Ephraim Masok, pastor of the Evangelical Church Winning All (ECWA) in the Rikkos area of Jos was killed in December 2010.
- Rev. Bulus Marwa, 37, pastor of Victory Baptist Church, was killed in Maiduguri.
- Pastor G. C Shawari, senior pastor with the Christ Apostolic Church, was killed in his church in Jos.
- Pastor Baba Ali Samari, 57, of the Good News Church, Maiduguri, was killed in his residence.
- Pastor Yahaya Wuro Buntu, 72, a Deeper Life pastor was killed in his uncompleted church in Bajoga Town, Gombe State.
- Pastor Michael Peter Yakwa of the Ekklesiyar Yan'uwa a Nigeria (EYN—the Church of the Brethren in Nigeria) was killed along with 10 members of his congregation in the Kwaple Church in the denomination's Chibok district, Borno State.
- Pastor Joseph Yari of ECWA was shot and killed in a Baptist Church in the Tudan Wada area of Jos.

What does this say to us? It says that there is danger in doing God's work. It also suggests that for the gospel to go forward, there must be sacrifice. All of us understand that there may be sacrifice required of us in order for the gospel to advance.

The Alamo

This is similar to the sacrifice that was made in order to conquer the Western part of the United States and particular Texas. Perhaps the most well known event in the history of Texas is the Battle for the Alamo. Texas declared its independence from Mexico on March 2, 1936. The rumblings of independence had been going on for months so about ten days before the declaration of independence General Antonio López de Santa Anna had already arrived at the Alamo with about 1500 troops to put down the rebellion. At that time the Alamo was being defended by about 100 Texans. Everyone knew the battle was coming and a few days before Santa Anna arrived two groups of defenders arrived, about 30 men led by Jim Bowie and a smaller group led by Davy Crockett. After Santa Anna arrived and surrounded the Alamo, 32 more men slipped into the fort. Also while the siege was going on, Davy Crockett led a small group of men outside and found another group that was willing to go back inside to help defend the Alamo. Every one of these people who entered that compound understood that there were very grave risks and likely death.

Colonel William Travis, commander of the small force at the Alamo, wrote a letter which he entitled "To the People of Texas and All Americans in the World." In the letter, Travis said, "I am determined to sustain myself as long as possible & die like a soldier who never forgets what is due to his own honor & that of his country. VICTORY OR DEATH."

The battle was joined in the early morning of March 6, 1936. Within seven hours or so, all of the defenders inside the Alamo except two had been killed. No one knows exactly how many people died. The estimate ranges from 182 to 257. When the fall of the Alamo was announced, instead of striking fear in the heart of the Texans as Santa Anna was convinced would happen, this galvanized and motivated the Texans. Hundreds volunteered to join the army of Sam Houston. On April 27, some six weeks later, Sam Houston's ragtag Texas army surprised and defeated the Mexican army and captured General Santa Anna. This bought time for the new Texas Republic which later became the 28th state of the United States.

Here is the point: If Texans were willing to go to such great lengths to defend their nation or their state—to the point of giving up their lives, how much more should we be willing to follow the example of Jesus and make whatever sacrifices are necessary to see God's kingdom advance on this earth.

Humility Today

What was the attitude of Jesus? It was one that was willing to yield up personal rights in order to rescue those who were far less deserving than he was.

- He gave up the right of the beauties and splendours and glories of heaven.
- He gave up the right of ownership of property. He only owned his clothes.
- He gave up the right of having a family.
- He gave up the right of being a "big man." He was even willing to wash his disciples' feet.
- He gave up the right to life itself.

The ultimate illustration of humility is that of Jesus. Paul wrote, *"Your attitude should be the same as that of Christ Jesus . . ."* Here was Jesus enjoying all the splendors and beauties and advantages of the perfect spiritual world but he freely and willingly gave up all those things in order to win humankind.

Paul stated that although he was by nature God, he did not consider that equality with God something to be held on to but..

> ... made himself nothing, taking the very nature of a servant, being made in human likeness. And being found in appearance as a man he humbled himself and became obedient to death—even death on a cross!
>
> —Phil. 2:8

What does all of this mean to us today?

Humility takes concern for the property of others.

Paul wrote that we are to look out after the *interests of others*. The interests of others include their property. Being interested in the rights of others might mean giving up your personal rights. Are you concerned about the property of other people?

A Pastor's Choice to Love or Not

Shortly after becoming the pastor of a church, a young man in the church came to inform me that he felt called to attend another church. I tried to discourage him but he eventually left and went to another church. However, since he lived in the same small town, we continued to have ongoing contact. Because we have cold weather in the winter season, we have to heat our houses. Some heat with gas; some heat with electricity but I was a bit old-fashioned and preferred to heat with wood.

One day I went into the bush and cut a load of firewood for my wood heater. As I was driving home, a thought came into my mind that this man who had left my church was very busy and did not have much wood for his wood heater. I resisted this thought because, first I had worked hard for that wood, and, second, if I were going to give the wood away, I was certainly not going to give it to such a traitor. However, I continued to wrestle with the thought that Jesus had taught us to love even our enemies and do good to those who had abused us. I could not get away from the thought so I turned and went to his house. There was no one at home but I dumped the whole load of firewood in his compound and left. I drove on to my house with an empty truck but a very full heart, a heart filled with joy because I had put someone else's interest ahead of my own. Whether this incident had anything to do with it or not, I do not know, but my straying church member did return to my church where he remained faithful until I left.

Humility is concerned about the feelings of others.

Not only should we be concerned about the property of others, we should also be concerned about their feelings.

This is the subject of Romans 14 which is in the practical part of the book where Paul is addressing some of the conflicts that were part of the young church—particularly disagreements over social and religious issues. Paul illustrates these by describing the different positions as the strong and the weak.

The first thing you must understand about this passage is that the "strong" and "weak" do not refer to new believers and older more mature believers. The strong conscience is one that does not bother the person very much. The "weak" person is the one whose conscience bothers him or her about the smallest things. The strong brother, the one whose conscience is strong enough to allow him to do more things, must not flaunt his liberties. Paul wrote, *"The man who eats everything must not look down on him who does not"* (14:3a). The weak brother, on the other hand, must not go around challenging the convictions of the strong. Romans 14:3b states, *"and the man who does not eat everything must not condemn the man who does, for God has accepted him."*

The illustration in this context has to do with eating. There are many issues where churches take different positions and even individuals within local churches take different positions. It has only been in the last few years that many churches have become "strong" enough to allow traditional African instruments back in the church. The consciences of some of the older Christians still associate the traditional instruments with the old religions and their consciences have a difficult time allowing them to worship where these instruments are being used.

Closely connected with this is the more informal and emotional styles of worship generated by Pentecostalism that are being carried over into other churches. Many of the older Christians are "weak" on those issues.

Conclusion

Missionaries are one group that is made up of strong-willed opinionated people. They are hard-working and committed. They are willing to live sacrificial lives. They are often quite successful at what they do. Therefore, it is sometimes difficult for them to be humble and submit themselves to someone who is not as committed, not as experienced and perhaps not as intelligent. However, God calls missionaries and others to that kind of humility.

Humility means that we are willing to yield up our rights in order not to offend those whose consciences are weaker than our own.

Have you developed the attitude of Christ? Are you practicing the humility that was illustrated by Jesus?

CHAPTER 9

OBEDIENCE

(2:12-13)

Therefore, my dear friends, as you have always obeyed—not only in my presence, but now much more in my absence—continue to work out your salvation with fear and trembling, for it is God who works in you to will and to act according to his good purpose.

—Phil. 2:12-13

Paul paid the Philippians a very high compliment in this paragraph. He commended them for their obedience. They were continuing to obey the precepts of Christianity even when Paul who had taught them such principles, was not there to supervise and insist on their obedience. Paul stated here that just as they have obeyed God in the past, they must continue to work out their salvation *"with fear and trembling."* I understand that statement to be a reference to obedience. The committed Christian believer is a person who is going to continue to obey God.

Although there is certainly no Christian who would encourage anyone to disobey, it seems that, at least in some circles, obedience does not receive the emphasis that it receives in the Bible. I am not sure why, but one possible reason is that we Protestants are so committed to the concept of justification by faith and we are so afraid of straying into the idea of somehow being justified by works that we have at times inadvertently reduced our stress on obedience to God. However, there are many instructions, commands, precepts and exhortations in the Bible that the Christian must obey.

Fortunately, obedience is not a very difficult concept to understand. It simply means doing what one has been told to do. It is submitting oneself to requirements of those in authority. All areas of life require obedience:

- Children must obey their parents.
- Athletes must obey their coaches.
- Students must obey their teachers.
- Workers must obey their employees.
- Citizens must obey their governments.
- Drivers must obey the rules of the highway.
- Soldiers must obey their commanding officers.

There is no society in the world that does not have the concept of obedience.

Obedience is certainly an important concept in the Bible. Here are some Biblical commands we need to obey:

- Command to Love. *"Love your neighbor as yourself"* (Leviticus 19:18; Matthew 22:39).
- Command to Forgive. *"If he [your brother]sins against you seven times in a day and seven times comes back to you and says, 'I repent,' forgive him"* (Luke 17:4).
- Command to Non-Violence. *"If someone strikes you on the right cheek, turn to him the other also"* (Matthew 5:39b).
- Command to Whole-Hearted Work. *"Whatever you do, work at it with all your heart, as working for the Lord"* (Colossians 3:23).

- Command to Submit to Authorities. *"Submit yourselves for the Lord's sake to every authority instituted among men"* (1 Peter 2:13).
- Command to Proper Communication. *"Do not let any unwholesome talk come out of your mouths, but only what is helpful for building others up according to their needs, that it may benefit those who listen"* (Ephesians 4:29).

I believe that the African worldview encourages obedience better than the Western independent-thinking mentality. Africans tend to have great respect for their leaders. Most Africans usually obey instantly and without question, even when they do not understand or even disagree with the command. They are so committed to the absolute rightness and authority of the senior person that obedience is almost unquestioned and automatic.

Recently I was traveling with my AIDS training team and James Ameh, one of my helpers, told a story that our team members kept talking about the rest of the trip. Here is the story:

> A soldier, driving a vehicle for his officer, took him to a hotel. While there the vehicle had a punctured tire so the officer told the driver to go repair the tire. A few minutes later, the security guards called the officer to come to the front of the hotel because there had been a confrontation between the driver and the security man. The security people were demanding some kind of paperwork before they would allow the vehicle to leave the hotel premises. All the soldier would say was, "Oga said, 'Go vulcanize the tire.'" That did not satisfy the security man so the soldier started beating the security man and shouting, "Oga said to go vulcanize the tire." Oga had given an order and there was no one who was going to interfere with his obedience of that very clear order.

Obviously that is an extreme example of unquestioned obedience. We certainly would not justify someone using violence in a situation like this. However, we Christians have something to learn from this soldier. All we need to know is what "Oga said." Once we know what Oga said, there should never be any hesitation in obedience.

Here are some questions for you to consider:

- Are you obeying the precepts of the Bible?
- Are you obeying the precepts of your church?
- Are you obeying what your conscience is telling you that you should be doing?
- Are you obeying what Oga said?

CHAPTER 10

SERVICE

(2:19-30)

Serving is perhaps the most basic aspect of a Christian's life. We have two examples given in Philippians 2.

The Example of Timothy (2:19-24)

Timothy was converted to Christ on Paul's first missionary journey and became Paul's traveling companion and assistant. He became an itinerant evangelist and later a pastor. In fact, Paul included him as one of the co-authors of the book to the Philippians. However, the fact that he now referred to him in the third person demonstrates that his inclusion as one of the co-authors was a demonstration of the partnership that Paul had with him and not a true example of co-authorship.

Note Paul's commentary on Timothy in verse 23: *"But you know that Timothy has proved himself, because as a son with his father he has served with me in the work of the gospel."*

The key word here is "served." This is the Greek word *douleo* and not *diakoneo*. Because slavery was so common, there were many words for the various kinds of servants. However, this one was the one that probably described the lowest of the group. It is the word most often translated simply as slave. Paul was saying here that Timothy was willing to work like a slave. He was commended here for his ministry, particularly for two aspects of it.

His Concern for the Philippians (2:20)

Paul wrote, *"I have no one else like him, who takes a genuine interest in your welfare."* Timothy loved the people among whom God had called him to work. One of the first and most important characteristics of genuine servants of God is they must love the people God has called them to serve. If you do not love the people you are called to serve, you are going to have a very limited success.

Earlier we have seen an illustration of the love that Paul had for the Philippians. It is wonderful that the same kind of love Paul had is now reflected by Timothy. He was a true disciple of Paul.

- Do you have genuine concern for the people you serve or are you just serving them until you get promoted?
- Do you enjoy being around the people of your congregation or ministry?
- Do you talk positively about your people when you are with your friends?
- Do you enjoy helping your people with their problems?
- Are you happy when you see one of your people in a distant place?
- Do you get angry when you hear the people you are serving being talked about negatively?

I love the people God has called me to serve. How do I know this? I enjoy being with them. When I see a Nigerian in the US, something in me feels good. Whenever I hear someone outside of Nigeria criticizing Nigeria, I feel angry. When friends visit Nigeria from the outside, I always encourage them to go back and say good things about Nigeria.

I am sure I do not have the capacity to love Nigeria like Timothy loved the Philippians but I am trying.

When you get to the place where you are focusing more on the faults and failures of the people you are serving, perhaps it is time for you to find another place to serve. If you are only tolerating the people that you are serving, maybe it is time for a break. This does not mean we do not get frustrated with those we serve. Even in our families, we get frustrated. However, that does not reduce our love for them and it is not something that lasts a long time.

Has God given you a special love for the people you serve? Could someone say about you, like Paul said of Timothy, there is no one else who loves these people like you do? That is one of the characteristics of a real servant of Jesus.

His Relationship with Paul (2:22)

Paul wrote, *"you know that Timothy has proved himself because as a son with his father he has served with me in the work of the gospel."* Not only did Timothy have a good relationship with the people he was serving but he had a good relationship with Paul, his colleague and superior.

I am sure you are aware that there is nothing that will rob you of your joy quicker than having a poor relationship with your fellow ministers and your spiritual authorities. I think it is equally true that nothing can produce greater joy than having a very good working relationship with your colleagues and superiors. Do you have a good relationship with your colleagues? If you do not, you are not going to have a very joyful ministry in your church.

The Example of Epaphroditus (2:25-30)

Epaphroditus was a layman in the church at Philippi. When the church heard Paul was in prison in Rome, they sent Epaphroditus to Paul to check on him and to serve as his personal assistant while he was in prison. He left his home to serve with a missionary. He was not a professionally trained missionary but a layman. He went to help relieve Paul of some of the routine things so Paul could focus on more important things. Epaphroditus had some qualities that are essential to be successful in one's ministry:

A Short-Term Missionary

In fact, Epaphroditus is an excellent example of a short-term missionary. He was not professionally trained to be a missionary and did not volunteer to serve permanently. He only agreed to serve in a limited fashion. He had all the qualities necessary to be a good short-term missionary.

- He was *worker* (2:25; a "fellow-worker"). This implies that he was not afraid of hard work. He was not lazy.
- He was *courageous* (2:25; "fellow soldier"). This figure of speech implies that he was tough.
- He was *faithful*. He delivered the message and stayed behind to serve Paul even though he was very sick.
- He was *submissive*. He is described here as a "messenger." That word is actually apostolos, meaning one who is sent by another. One who is sent by another is under the authority of the one doing the sending.
- He was *committed* (2:30; "risking his life"). He even risked his life to fulfill the task that the church had given him.

These are the qualities necessary to be a successful missionary or Christian worker.

- *You have to be a hard worker.* If you cannot work hard, you should not go into any kind of Christian ministry. Successful Christian workers like to work hard.
- *You have to be tough, like a soldier.* There are many obstacles you must overcome if you are to be successful in your ministry. You have to be tough because there will be many people who abuse you and misunderstand you and fail to appreciate the sacrifice you are making.
- *You have to be faithful.* Not all of us can be bishops or chairmen or administrators. However, all of us can carry messages. All of us can do something and we must be faithful in what God gives us to do.
- *You have to be submissive.* Epaphroditus was a man under authority. All Christian workers and leaders must likewise be submissive to their authorities. To fail to be submissive implies a spirit of independence and this is not the spirit of Christ.
- *You must be committed.* If you are not committed to your task and to be successful in your ministry, there will be plenty temptations to quit. However, a strong dose of commitment will keep you on the job.

Whether we like it or not, the Church is utilizing more short-term missionaries. I am not sure of all of the reasons why and it really does not matter. What does matter is that most modern mission agencies are going to use the services of more people who are only committed to a limited time of service. We can do two things about this:

- We can complain.
- We can work with them.

Short-Term Missions Projects

It is obvious that the short-term missionary is normally not going to be as successful as the career missionary. However, short-term missionaries can be effective. What are some specific things that missionary teams can do?

Construction Projects

One of the most effective ways short-term missionaries can be used is in building projects. Even a person who does not have a specific skill can participate in a project like this. This gives the person some good exposure to the mission field, along with a positive sense of accomplishment.

As a pastor, I led a small team of men from my church to Alaska to work on a building project. Some have gone back to Alaska several times to work on other mission projects. And I can assure you that these workers have a great love for the missionaries working in Alaska and support them greatly. That first exposure to missions in Alaska changed them and, to some extent, changed the church as well.

Medical Projects

Many doctors and other health professionals volunteer to go to the mission field. They can be involved in training, relieving an overworked missionary or doing medical outreach or clinics in remote areas. They will usually enjoy the experience and are normally of great assistance.

Evangelistic Teams

Doing evangelism in a cross-cultural situation is more difficult than doing construction because often there are different languages and certainly different cultures involved. However, with some good preparation, a church could put together an effective evangelistic team to send to the mission field. With media like the Jesus Film and technical tools, short-term missionaries can be of genuine assistance to the missionary.

One organization that has used this strategy effectively is Teen Missions, which recruits, prepares and sends American teenagers on mission trips during their school holidays. Three of my nieces have participated in these projects. They usually work on a construction project along with evangelistic outreaches using drama, music or sports or conducting a Vacation Bible School. The students are carefully trained and carefully coordinated. Teen Missions helps missionaries but the most important thing they do is give young people positive exposure to the mission field.

A church does not need to wait until some organization comes along to show them what to do. Many churches are very capable of putting together a group of students or adults to work on a mission field for two or three weeks.

I have worked with two short-term missionary projects that have been very successful.

A Florida Video Team

A few years ago, I became convinced that I needed to move in the direction of doing more video work. If I can put some of the things that I do on video, then that will relieve me from having to go in person to all these places. I convinced my pastor in the US of the value of this project. This church has a TV ministry and a good group of technical people who understand video technology. They sent over a team of seven who spent two and a half weeks training our local people. It was a perfect short-term missionary project. They actually did something that could not be done in Nigeria so they supplied a real need. And they also received a real vision for the ministry in Nigeria.

An Amazing Short-Term Missionary

A few years ago, the Lord sent over Dr. Ron Rice to help us. He came for a three and a half month period. Now, let me describe some of the things that he has helped us do.

- He has worked on five of the six CRK *Teachers' Manuals*, doing practically all of the research, much of the writing, all of the editing and all of the work getting permission to use various articles in our manuals. This is a project that I created but it would not have gone very far if I did not have someone else to help me.
- He has helped to create a ministry to handicapped people. This ministry has given out over 2600 wheelchairs in the last eight years to needy people.
- He has edited all of my recent books and the books of several Nigerians.
- He has purchased and delivered many ministry tools for Nigerian missionaries including video projectors, portable DVD players and laptop computers.
- He assists Africa Christian Textbooks (ACTS) by helping to buy books and helping with emergency shipping.
- He has served as a consultant to others who are going to serve overseas on a short-term basis.
- He has raised money for several different kinds of ministries in Nigeria.
- His wife, Sharon, sometimes comes over with him and spends a month working with my wife, Mary, on various projects that she needs to get done around the house.

Ron Rice lives in Seattle, Washington, USA ten months out of the year. However, he does the work and supervises the work of many full-time missionaries. Ron Rice is a good Epaphroditus. He is a successful short-term missionary.

Summary

The modern world tends to focus on fun and adventure. Many people live for the weekend. They spend their money on buying things that will give them prestige and status. When these people get together, all they often talk about is football and movies and other rather nonessential activities. However, God has called his workers to a much higher calling—to service for God. This is an exalted position. We are co-laborers with Christ.

CHAPTER 11

CAREFULNESS

(3:1-4)

Watch out for those dogs, those men who do evil, those mutilators of the flesh. For it is we who are the circumcision, we who worship by the Spirit of God

—Phil. 3:2-4

A Philippian Problem

Some time after Paul planted the church in Philippi, there crept into the church the same or similar group to those who had attacked the Galatian churches. These were apparently Jewish Christians who were demanding that if Gentiles wanted to become genuine Christians they had to essentially become Jews. The thing they particularly stressed was the need for Gentile men to be circumcised before they could be fully welcomed into the family of God.

Fortunately, the battle over circumcision had already been fought and won at the Jerusalem Council as described in Acts 15. These *"mutilators of the flesh"* were bad losers. They were continuing to insist on their interpretation of the Law even though the church had already officially rejected their position and published and distributed their decision to those affected by them. This should have settled the issue once and for all but there were still dissenters.

Paul warned the Philippian church against this divisive and self-centered group of people and told the Philippians that they should be careful in interacting with them and other such people. This group was obviously demanding what God did not demand and as such were creating stumbling blocks for the new Gentile believers. They were fellow human beings and they were also fellow Christians in some sense of the word. However, they represented a danger that needed to be guarded against.

Several years before this epistle was written the issue of circumcision had already been settled. Therefore, it is not necessary to spend much time on that. However, there are two specific applications that come from this issue that are worth noting.

Two Points of Application

Followers of Jesus must be vigilant to make sure no heresy perverts the gospel.

I believe there is a good bit of flexibility within the Christian faith for the application of various truths. For example, in Romans 14, we learn that there were some Christians who set apart one day as a special day of worship and another group who treated every day the same way. The issue of setting aside one day as holy or not was not a big issue to Paul. Both groups were within the boundaries of Christian practice. In such things, Paul wanted all Christians to be fully convinced in their own minds and to make sure they kept the convictions of their own conscience (Romans 14:5).

However, it was possible to claim to be a Christian and step across the line—to go too far and to make Christian belief and practice something that it is not, and in so doing, pervert the faith. This is what Paul was trying to warn against. Although he pleaded for tolerance of each other, he was not tolerant of heresy. And attempting to mix the old religious practice of circumcision with Christian faith, to Paul and to the rest of the early church, was going too far. It was confusing the Gentiles. It was undermining one of the basic tenets of the Christian faith. Therefore, Paul encouraged the Philippians to be watchful and careful of anyone who would attempt to do this.

There is one issue in Nigeria that illustrates this natural human tendency of marrying the old religions with the new religions. In many of our churches in Nigeria today, the "blood of Jesus" is constantly being referred to or used. When people get sick, someone will pray for them and "sprinkle the blood of Jesus" on them. When people travel, someone will "sprinkle the blood of Jesus" on the vehicle. Of course all of this is done in a metaphorical sense.

The essential part of most traditional African religions was protection—protection from evil spirits, protection from unhappy ancestors, protection from other kinds of evil forces. So one of the essential parts of traditional religions was to appease and satisfy these spiritual forces. There was little stress on justice and righteousness and almost no emphasis on loving the gods. The main thing was to protect oneself and try to secure their blessings. Therefore, when one of the spirits or one of the ancestors supposedly became angry, one might kill a chicken or a goat or make some other kind of sacrifice that would hopefully appease this offended spirit. The bigger the sacrifice the more likely the offended spirit would be appeased.

The blood of Jesus is an important part of Christian theology. It is the symbol for the death of Christ which is the foundation upon which all of the benefits of our faith are provided. The death of Christ in some way appeased the wrath of God and allows him to be just in releasing us from the penalty our sin deserves. In an indirect way, then, the death of Christ also provides all the other benefits that we enjoy as Christians.

However, in many Christian circles, the blood of Jesus has become that means to ward off sickness and accidents and injuries and attacks on our family and other misfortunes of life. Biblical support is found in the story of the deliverance from Egypt when the death angel passed over the homes of the Israelites after seeing the blood on the doorpost. However, the blood of Jesus is not an agent or talisman or fetish to protect us from the misfortunes of life and we must be very careful not to allow our people to get that impression.

The use of the blood of Jesus as a protecting agent confuses the teachings of the Bible about our protection and about the significance of the death of Christ. The blood of Jesus represents the death of Jesus and the death of Jesus is what satisfies the justice of God related to our sin. God has provided another means to protect us. The Bible says that God has prepared his angels as the primary means of providing protection for his people (Psalm 91:11; Daniel 6:22; Luke 4:10; Hebrews 1:14).

Is this a serious problem? I do not think that it reaches the level of heresy. In fact, I think our God is a very gracious God. He hears us when we pray and interprets the prayers of our hearts and grants us what we need, even when we do not ask properly.

However, we must learn to be careful. We who are teachers and preachers and disciplers and are most experienced in our Christian faith must be watchful and careful and not wait until something has developed into a full-fledged heresy. We must be there to guide our people and steer them away from anything that would potentially weaken or compromise their faith.

To be honest, protecting the church against heresy is not one of the most joyful tasks of the church leader. Few people enjoy opposing heresy though it needs to be done. There is no joy in the process but it makes joy possible later.

Preserving a Church from Heresy

When I was the pastor of a church in southern Georgia, I met an African-American layman whose church had recently gone though some of the same problems that my church had experienced before I had arrived. I got to know him quite well and he invited me to meet his pastor and to listen to his choir. Soon the man told me about another white man who had been very friendly to the church. I soon met this other white man and learned that he was a disciple of Sun Myung Moon. It was my most sober responsibility to take the leading layman aside and explain to him who this man was and what they believed and what they would do to his church. I am happy to report that the church eventually severed their relationship with this man who was attempting to promote a perverted type of Christianity.

This is not the place to try to precisely define Christian doctrine and to attempt to outline every possible type of heresy. Perhaps the biggest danger we face in Nigeria is syncretism, not unlike what the early church faced. The Jewish Christians were very tempted to mix their new faith with their old faith. There was a considerable overlap between the traditional Jewish faith and the Christian faith and that was fine. However, where there was divergence, the differences had to be recognized, the distinctives of the Christian faith and practice had to be preserved and the non-conforming Jewish practices rejected.

Syncretism is a big danger. It is something that pastors and even laypeople should be looking for constantly. There are many things we can learn and use from our past cultures. However, we must not step across the line to the point that our worship of God gets confused with the former worship of idols.

I do not have a checklist that you can use to guarantee theological purity. However, the best defense against heresy is a strong offense—a clear focus on Jesus Christ and the clear teaching of God's Word. Therefore, I think perhaps the most essential thing we can do avoid heresy is teach the Word of God plainly. Let us be careful that we do not allow theological error to creep into our church.

Followers of Jesus must not require new believers to participate in practices that are simply cultural or personal-religious preferences.

There was nothing wrong with circumcision. This was a Jewish religious practice that had become a cultural practice. Paul never forbade the Jews from practicing it. The practice of circumcision did have serious religious meaning in the Jewish culture. However, Paul insisted that it had nothing to do with Christianity and refused to demand it of the Gentile converts. In fact, he seriously opposed anyone who would demand circumcision of others.

There are many principles that transcend cultures and are observed the same way in nearly all cultures. Principles like honesty and sexual morality and the sacredness of life are practiced about the same everywhere. However, there are many other principles that work out very differently in different cultures. Even some of the basic principles are applied differently. The principle of respect for parents and authority is practiced much differently in various parts of the world. What is regarded as modest clothing varies from culture to culture. The styles of worship and singing and praying are different in different places.

We recognize that mistakes have been made in the past by missionaries who were more successful in Westernizing than

Christianizing their converts. I am not among those who are constantly criticizing the earlier missionaries who came to Africa. I have nothing but respect for them. They started a Christian revolution that has been perhaps the greatest success story in the history of Christianity. However, did they get the polygamy issue right by refusing to allow polygamist to be baptized or take communion? Were they right in associating the traditional musical instruments with the old religions and requiring Western hymns and styles of music? Were they right in ignoring the need for their Christian converts to be involved in politics and governance?

The Pineapple Story

Otto Konig tells the story in his book, *The Pineapple Story*, about paying a villager to plant pineapples and having difficulty with them being stolen. He eventually learned that it was the person who planted them who was taking them. However, the villagers explained that in their culture, the person who planted something was entitled to eat it. Konig learned a valuable lesson about giving the pineapples to God that later caused the people to stop taking them. However, Konig has also been criticized for failing to understand the cultural expectations in that village. All through the book, Konig insisted that the pineapples belonged to him and that the people in that village were thieves.

Perhaps the real offense here was a cultural offense—the fact that missionary failed to understand the worldview of the local people. Certainly stealing is contrary to Scripture. However, what constitutes ownership and what constitutes stealing vary from culture to culture.

Before we become too dogmatic about social and cultural issues, we need to make sure we have a very good understanding of the culture. We must not be guilty of imposing our own particular narrow cultural view on a moral or ethical issue. Getting the right balance in social and cultural issues requires great care.

CHAPTER 12

INTIMACY

(3:4-11)

The Value of Knowing Christ

Who we know is important. When he was very small, my son, Daniel, asked me on one occasion, "Dad, do you know Billy Graham?" Daniel assumed that if I knew an important person, that would mean that somehow I must also be important. I have met some important Christian leaders in my life, including Billy Graham and John Stott but to say that I know them in any kind of real personal way would not be accurate.

Paul outlined all of his assets as a well-trained Jewish rabbi in Philippians 3:4-6. These assets would have made him the envy of practically any Jew.

- 3:5a, properly circumcised on the eighth day
- 3:5b, an Israelite
- 3:5c, of the tribe of Benjamin
- 3:5d, *"a Hebrew of the Hebrews;"* This meant he was a strict Hebrew. If one said he was "an Igbo of the Igbos" we would understand that.

- 3:5e, as far as the law was concerned, a Pharisee. No more needed to be said. All Pharisees kept the law very strictly.
- 3:6a, his zeal was proved by his persecution of the church that threatened to weaken Judaism.
- 3:6b, a summary: As far as legalistic righteousness was concerned, Paul was "blameless." No one could find fault with him.

However, after encountering Christ, Paul found something that was more valuable than all of these other things. Note the different ways he describes how cheap and worthless these assets and deeds were compared to his relationship with Christ.

- *"Whatever was to my profit I now consider loss for the sake of Christ"* (3:7). None of these things were as valuable as knowing Christ.
- *"What is more, I consider everything a loss compared to the surpassing greatness of knowing Christ Jesus my Lord, for whose sake I have lost all things"* (3:8).
- *"I consider them [all his accomplishments in Judaism] rubbish, that I may gain Christ and be found in him"* (3:8-9).

What was it that made Paul feel so low and worthless? It was the fact that he had met Jesus and viewing himself in comparison with Jesus made him feel like nothing. Knowing Christ was the most important thing in his life. All else compared to that was nothing.

A Policeman "Forgives" An "Offense"

Once when I was in Port Harcourt, I was arrested for not having seat belts on (the current law requiring seat belts to be worn in Nigeria was still ten years in the future). A plain clothes policeman and a soldier got in the vehicle with me. They said they wanted to take me to the police headquarters on Moscow Road.

Because I knew I had not committed any offense, I was quite relaxed about the incident. As we were going, I casually asked them if they knew a certain man. The policeman looked a bit shocked and said, "Do you know him?" I said, "Yes, we can drive straight to his house if you like." The policeman decided it was not necessary for us to continue on to Moscow Road because the person I had mentioned was the Rivers State Police Commissioner. The fact I knew him discouraged my adversaries from pursuing the case any further. He quickly changed from being an antagonist to a friend, based upon who I knew.

Paul was stating that all the good things, including the religious things he had done in the past were not nearly as valuable as knowing Christ.

How Do We Get to Know Someone?

All of us have friends. When we analyze how those people went from being strangers to becoming friends and even close friends, we observe several important things.

- *There must be an introduction.* You do not get to know someone very well by reading about him or her in a book. There must be a meeting.
- *There must be interaction.* You do not get to know someone by just greeting him or her one time. Most of us can remember times when we met important people. We might remember even the specific words that he or she said to us. However, those kinds of brief greetings do not help us to get to really know someone. There must be interaction. There must be give and take. There must be questions and answers. There must be conversation.
- *There must be repetition.* You do not get to know someone just meeting him or her one time. To say that you know someone implies that there have been a series of meetings.

- *There must be variation.* Some people have worked together in a factory for 20 years. However, they have known each other only in one setting, but never in a home or in a recreational setting or in a worship service. To really get to know a person, we need to interact regularly in a variety of settings.

It takes time to get to know someone. And it takes a certain kind of interactive, repetitive, variable kind of time. I have sat next to people on an airplane for eight hours but afterwards I could not even tell you what country they came from.

Some time ago, I had the privilege of speaking at the Aso Rock Villa Chapel, the chapel that then President Obasanjo had built and where he worshipped every Sunday while he was the president. People since that time have said, "I did not know you knew the president." This is one of those situations where you have to define the word "know" quite well. I met the president when he was in the Jos prison. I go there and preach occasionally and met him while he was a political prisoner there. After that, I sent him some books to read. After he became president, I have been with him on several different occasions.

After I had preached at the Aso Rock Chapel, my son, Daniel, videoed an interview with the president. As Daniel was setting up his equipment, he introduced himself to the president as "Danny McCain's son." The president said, "Oh, that is good. Dr. McCain is my good friend. He told a naughty story about you in his sermon a couple of weeks ago." The bottom line is I know former President Obasanjo and he knows me. We are "friends" in some sense of the word. However, I really do not know him intimately. I do not know him well enough to predict what he is going to do next. I do not know him well enough to understand his facial expressions and attitudes. I do not know him like I know my colleagues at the University of Jos.

Obviously it makes an average person feel quite good when an important person knows him or her. We like to drop into our conversations the fact that we are friends with a certain "big" person. However, often these are only casual relationships not real friendships.

What we want to make sure of is that we really know Jesus. We have met him. We have spent time with him. We have interacted with him. We have interacted with him in a variety of different ways. We have interacted with him enough that we really know him. We can tell when he is happy and when he is not happy. We enjoy being in his presence and believe he also enjoys it when we choose to spend time with him. That is what it means to know Jesus.

The Results of Knowing Christ

What are the results or benefits of knowing someone? If I know the man selling rice at the market very well, he may give me a fuller measure. If I know the president of the bank, I might be able to get a loan easier. If I know a sports figure, he may give me complimentary tickets to the next important match. Everyone we know brings to us certain benefits and blessings. What are the benefits of knowing Christ?

We will experience the righteousness of Christ.

> *What is more, I consider everything a loss compared to the surpassing greatness of knowing Christ Jesus my Lord, for whose sake I have lost all things. I consider them rubbish, that I may gain Christ and be found in him, not having a righteousness of my own that comes from the law, but that which is through faith in Christ—the righteousness that comes from God and is by faith.*
>
> —Phil. 3:8-9

One result of knowing Christ is not having a righteousness that comes from myself but that which comes from Christ. This is a righteousness that results from faith in Christ, not from keeping the law. To stress this point, Paul stated essentially the same thing two different times. He wrote, *"the righteousness that comes from God and is by faith."*

We could be just before God if we could keep the whole law. Unfortunately, all of us have already broken God's law and none of us can keep it perfectly. Thus, righteousness through keeping the law is impossible. God, recognizing our dilemma, decided to do something about it. He allowed Jesus to live a perfect sinless life and to die on the cross. This satisfied the justice of God with regards to our sin. God decreed if we would put our trust in Christ, if we would accept the gift that he had provided for us and reject all other attempts at being righteous, he would accept our faith as the basis for righteousness. We are therefore not declared righteous on the basis of our keeping the law or good deeds but on the basis of our faith in Christ's atonement for us. This is the good news of the gospel.

We will experience the power of Christ.

Paul wrote, *"I want to know Christ and the power of his resurrection"* (the resurrection kind of power). How powerful is Christ?

- He was powerful enough to turn water into wine.
- He was powerful enough to heal the sick.
- He was powerful enough to drive away demons.
- He was powerful enough to feed 5000 people with one boy's lunch.
- He was powerful enough to stop a raging storm.
- He was powerful enough to be raised from the dead.

Why do we need the power of Christ? We do not need it to show off how powerful we are.

- We need the power of Christ to help us live victoriously over sin.
- We need the power of Christ to help us witness and win unbelievers to Christ.
- We need the power of Christ to help us to lead those under our ministry.
- We need the power of Christ to help us live up to the difficult teachings of Jesus.
- We need the power of Christ to overcome the powers of Satan.
- We need the power of Christ to manifest itself in our lives and demonstrate that God is more powerful than Satan.

Many of my Pentecostal friends have gone too far on the issue of power while many of my non-Pentecostal friends have retreated too far in the other direction. Is Jesus still the same yesterday, today and forever? Did Jesus not say that we would do greater and more things than even he did? Where are the greater things we are supposed to do?

Miracles are not on every page of the Bible. There seemed to be seasons of miracles—times when God was doing something special. I believe the same thing is true today. I believe that there are seasons of miracles. God allows miracles in our lives to demonstrate his resurrection power and to help substantiate that he is the God of truth.

On one occasion, one of my students went to a remote village in the bush to collect data for a missionary organization. The only person in the village who could speak Hausa was a 12-year old boy. This boy took my student to the chief and then left. Unfortunately, the chief could not speak Hausa. Thus my friend had no ability to communicate with him. The chief called the other chiefs and they tried to communicate with the young missionary. Unfortunately, there was no common language in which they could communicate. The missionary observed that these chiefs were getting more and more agitated. Finally he heard one of them say, "We do not know who this young man is. Maybe he was sent to spy out our land and he is going to come back with a force to kill us and capture our land." The missionary quickly replied, "No, I am not that kind of person. I am here doing research."

Suddenly he realized he was talking to them in their language, a language that he did not know and had never heard. For the next three hours, he gathered all the information he needed, in their language! The chiefs asked him which of their villages he had come from. My friend told them he was from southern Kaduna. They said, "No, your father must be from our place. You speak our language like we do."

After he left the meeting and was walking in the village, he met someone on the path and could not even think of the greeting in their language. The material he gathered during that interview was later reviewed by local people and deemed to be correct. That young man had experienced the power of Christ!

We will experience the suffering of Christ.

We love to think about the power of Christ but Paul also wrote: *"I want to know Christ . . . and the fellowship of sharing in his sufferings"* (3:10). Paul understood that a true identity with Christ—the ability to know Christ in an intimate way—would mean we must experience the same kinds of things that Jesus had experienced. Though martyrdom never became an every day occurrence in the early church period, it became so well known that the early church recognized and prepared its members for such a possibility. Peter wrote:

> *To this you were called, because Christ suffered for you, leaving you an example that you should follow in his steps . . . When they hurled their insults at him, he did not retaliate; when he suffered, he made no threats. Instead, he entrusted himself to him who judges justly.*
> —1 Peter 2:21-23

Have you ever been ridiculed because of your identification with Christ? Have you ever suffered because of your Christian faith? All of this is part of knowing Christ.

What kinds of ways did Jesus suffer?

Misunderstanding

Jesus was misunderstood by his disciples who were quite dull at times. He was misunderstood by his family who really did not understand who he was. He was certainly misunderstood by Jewish religious leaders. They totally misunderstood his mission. One of the most difficult things in the world is to be misunderstood—to have your *"good spoken evil of."*

Rejection

Jesus' hometown rejected him. The religious leaders rejected him. Even one of his twelve disciples rejected him. Following Jesus is going to mean that we face rejection at times.

Loss

Jesus did not have many possessions on the earth to lose. However, he eventually lost the robe that was on his back.

Paul wrote,

> *Whatever was to my profit I now consider loss for the sake of Christ. What is more, I consider everything a loss compared to the surpassing greatness of knowing Christ Jesus my Lord.*
> —Phil. 3:7-8

Many Christians have lost all their possessions because of following Jesus.

Physical Suffering

The suffering Jesus experienced leading up to the cross and while he was on the cross is almost unimaginable. It has been realistically portrayed in Mel Gibson's movie "The Passion of the Christ." Some may have suffered a bit for our faith but few if any have ever suffered the way Jesus suffered.

If we are called on to suffer physically, we should take comfort in the fact that we are sharing with Jesus in his suffering.

Death

The natural conclusion to suffering is death. This was true with Jesus. He eventually suffered to the point his body could not survive and he died.

Jesus said that the enemy comes to *"steal and kill and destroy"* (John 10:10). Paul declares that the last enemy to be conquered will be death (1 Corinthians 15:26). For reasons we do not fully understand, God calls some people to face this enemy before they would have died naturally. If we are called on to do so, we can be assured that we are identifying with Jesus in his death.

Observations from the Jos Crisis

During the Jos Crisis in September 2001, when mobs were roving the city burning and killing and the university was under attack, there was once when we got our passports and locked the house up. A few hours later I recorded my thoughts during that experience in my journal:

> In fact, this was one of the most emotional moments of the entire crisis up to that point. I had not had time to think too much about the worst case scenarios. However, when I ran upstairs and got those passports, just before I walked out of the bedroom, I turned and looked at this wonderful place I had lived in for ten years. The bed was there. Everything was very

familiar and in its place. I ran downstairs and got the computers from my office. I looked at my books in the bookshelves and my degrees hanging on the wall and all the things piled up on my desk. I wondered if I would ever see them again. I ran outside and handed the two computers to Michael who was sitting in the back seat and did not even have time to hug Mary goodbye. I turned away with the thought in my mind, "Is this the last time I will ever see my family? Is it possible that this could be the end?" For one fleeting moment, the thought crossed my mind that perhaps I should get in that vehicle and go with the others. However, I knew my place was to remain behind with the boys at the house. Those thoughts were fleeting and momentary but they were real. There was one other very brief thought that I had as I stood there beside that Jeep with its engine running and Mary inside and me on the outside. The thought went like this. "If this is it, I have no regrets. I am grateful that I have been able to serve God in Nigeria."

We will experience the resurrection of Christ.

Paul concluded this paragraph about knowing Christ, *"and so, somehow, to attain to the resurrection from the dead"* (3:11). Paul understood if he really knew Christ, he had hope of being raised from the dead. If Paul knew Christ and Christ knew Paul, Christ would certainly not allow Paul to remain in the clutches of death because death was going to be the last enemy to be conquered.

Easter is the most joyful time of the Christian calendar. The resurrection of Jesus is what sets Christianity apart from all other religions. The resurrection is an important part of the doctrine of the atonement. It is that which completes the process of providing salvation for us. However, it is also a beacon light shining to us of what our own future resurrection will be like.

Do you know Christ? Do you consider knowing Christ more valuable than anything else in the world? This was Paul's ambition and should be the desire of all who follow Jesus.

CHAPTER 13

SPIRITUAL PROGRESS

(3:12-14)

Paul had accomplished many things in his life.

- He had received a special call from Jesus.
- He had experienced additional revelations and visions from Jesus.
- He had been selected by Jesus and the church to take the gospel to the Gentiles.
- He had already completed three missionary tours by the time he wrote Philippians.
- He had planted several churches and won thousands of converts.
- He had trained a number of Christian leaders.
- He had written material that was to become part of the Holy Bible.
- He had become the *de facto* leader of the worldwide followers of Jesus.

There is no other Christian who had ever accomplished so much in such a short period of time as the Apostle Paul. Yet here is his testimony:

> Not that I have already obtained all this, or have already been made perfect, but I press on to take hold of that for which Christ Jesus took hold of me.
>
> —Phil. 3:12

Paul was not satisfied to remain where he was. He wanted to continue growing into the image and likeness of Jesus. He continued his challenging testimony and essentially repeated himself:

> Brothers, I do not consider myself yet to have taken hold of it. But one thing I do: forgetting what is behind and straining toward what is ahead, I press on toward the goal to win the prize for which God has called me heavenward in Christ Jesus.
> —Phil. 3:13-14

What is the significance of those personal statements? What do they tell us about Paul's view of his own spiritual growth and progress?

Paul Focused on Improvement rather than Attainment.

Two times in these two sections, Paul makes essentially the same statement:

- Not that I have already obtained all this.
- I do not consider myself yet to have taken hold of it.

These statements suggest that Paul was not satisfied with where he was. He constantly felt the need for growth and development.

God has designed us human beings in such a way that we must continually be growing. And if we are to be well-rounded Christian believers, that growth must be wholesome growth or growth in all parts of our being.

We must continue to *grow mentally*. We must continue to learn. Mental growth produces a lot of joy. "*It is the glory of God to conceal a matter; to search out a matter is the glory of kings*" (Proverbs 25:2). God cannot learn anything; therefore he gets glory out of concealing things from the creatures he has made and watching them seek them out. The highest thing a person can do, even if he is a king, is to search out and discover and uncover new truths. Learning is one of the greatest sources of joy.

This is why preaching and teaching is such a great blessing to me. I have to learn a lot before I can pass anything along to others. If a person stops growing mentally, that person is as good as dead.

We must continue to *grow spiritually*. As well as Paul knew Jesus, he recognized a need to know him better. Regardless of how much we know Christ and how committed and sanctified we are, there is always room for growth. None of us is in a place where we can relax.

- Are you growing spiritually?
- Are you continuing to learn more about prayer?
- Are you continuing to read and learn from God's word?
- Are you continuing to draw closer to God and learning more about what pleases God and honors Him?
- Are you closer to God this year than you were this time last year?

Paul Focused on the Future rather than the Past.

"Forgetting what is behind and straining toward what is ahead, I press on toward the goal" (3:13-14a). If most of us had accomplished ten per cent of what Paul had done, I am afraid we would be satisfied to sit around and bask in the sunlight of our accomplishments. However, that was not Paul's personality. He was not really interested in telling stories about the past. He was interested in stretching out to accomplish more in the future.

Someone once asked a small boy what he wanted to be when he grew up and he replied, "A returned missionary." That is the attitude of many people. They would love to be able to tell the missionary stories but they do not want to go through all that it took to gather those stories. Fortunately, Paul was much more motivated by future opportunities than past successes. He did not want to go through life just remembering the previous blessings. He wanted to experience new challenges and create new opportunities to know Christ and do his work.

I return to the US twice a year and while there, I do public relations work for our organization. I love to tell the stories of what God has done for our organization during our short history. But the thing that really motivates me is the opportunities we have to spread the gospel through the public universities. The opportunities of the future are a much greater motivator to me than the few successes I have experienced in the past.

- Are you growing mentally?
- Are you reading books?
- Are you attending workshops and doing things that will expand your mind?
- Are you growing spiritually?
- How is your prayer life?
- Are you spending time studying the word of God for your own spiritual growth?
- Are you growing professionally? Are you doing your job better now than last year?

There is something blessed and joyful about looking back and recognizing you have grown, that you have improved, and that you are making spiritual progress.

Paul Focused on Christ Rather than Obstacles

The language Paul uses here is the language of struggle. He says that he is "pressing on." This implies that there are obstacles in the road that are trying to keep him from attaining his goal. What were some of those obstacles?

- Jewish persecution
- Roman detention
- Pagan opposition
- Christian misinterpretation
- Leadership confusion

However, in spite of all those things, Paul kept focused on Jesus. In verse 12 he says *"I press on to take hold of that for which Christ Jesus took hold of me."* Jesus had called Paul and had "taken hold" of him. Therefore, Paul was committed to making sure that he fulfilled what Jesus wanted him to do.

In verse 14, Paul says, *"I press on toward the goal to win the prize for which God has called me heavenward in Christ Jesus."* The prize that Paul was drawn toward was "in Christ Jesus." It was the prize that Christ had set for him.

The point I want to make is that the center of Paul's life and ministry was Jesus Christ. The only goal and the only prize that he was interested in was the one associated with Christ. All of the obstacles and all of the pain and all of the suffering were mere distractions. Paul failed to allow those things to capture his attention. Rather he kept pressing on to the goal that Christ Jesus had set for him.

There is an important lesson for us to learn from Paul. Life is filled with obstacles and difficulties and pressures. However, if we are to obtain the goal that Jesus has set for us, we must kept our eyes focused on Jesus and keep our ears tuned to the voice of the Holy Spirit. We must not allow distractions to break that gaze.

Summary

Paul was a person who continued to grow all throughout his life. He was a person who was not satisfied with the status quo. He always had a goal in mind. And that goal had been set for him by Jesus Christ.

We, too, must make sure that we too are pressing toward the goal that God has set for us and not allow ourselves to be distracted by the accomplishments of the past or the obstacles of the present.

CHAPTER 14

MATURITY

(3:15-16)

This point is similar to the previous one and certainly a logical outgrowth of it. However, I want to expand it just a bit. Paul began this paragraph, *"All of us who are mature should take such a view of things . . ."*

The word translated mature in this verse is teleios. Pythogoras, a famous Greek philosopher, divided his students into two categories —beginners and the *teleieos*—the mature. The word referred not to students who knew everything but to those who had progressed to the point that they were mature and sincere students. The word teleios refers to that which carries out the purpose for which it was designed.

Using Sunglasses for a Spoon

I often tell my students I can use my sunglasses to eat my breakfast in the morning but that is not the purpose for which they were made. It is only as I clean them off and put them on my eyes on a bright day that I am using them for the purpose for which they were designed. My sunglasses do not magnify things. However, I cannot find fault with them for not magnifying things because they were not made for that purpose.

Christians were designed to have fellowship with God. It is only as we learn to worship and have that fellowship that we can be mature Christians, those capable of doing what God called us to do. Paul concluded this paragraph by saying, *"Only let us live up to what we have already attained"* (3:16).

When you were a child, you looked forward to becoming an adult. You longed for the day when you would be tall and strong and make your own decisions and get a job and make your own money.

Although there is always room for growth, I believe that there is a level of spiritual growth in which it could be said that a person is a spiritual adult. That is what Paul meant when he wrote, *"all of us who are mature."*

We Should Have Characteristics of Maturity.

What are the characteristics of those who might be considered mature believers? The following scriptures suggest at least part of the answer:

- *Overflowing love.* "May the Lord make your love increase and overflow for each other and for everyone else, just as ours does for you" (1 Thessalonians 3:12) *"And I pray that you, being rooted and established in love may have power together with all the saints, to grasp how wide and long and high and deep is the love of Christ, and to know this love that surpasses knowledge."* (Ephesians 3:17b-19a).
- *Strong hearts.* "May he strengthen your hearts . . ."(1 Thessalonians 3:13a); *"I pray that out of his glorious riches he may strengthen you with power through his Spirit in the inner being . . ."* (Ephesians 3:16).
- *Blameless character.* " . . . so that you will be blameless and holy in the presence of our God and Father when our Lord Jesus comes with all his holy ones"(1 Thessalonians 3:13b); *"May your whole spirit, soul and body be kept blameless at the coming of our Lord Jesus Christ."* (5:23b).

- *Inner holiness.* "*May God himself, the God of peace, sanctify you through and through. May your whole spirit, soul and body be kept blameless at the coming of our Lord Jesus Christ*"(5:23).
- *Christ inside.* "*. . .so that Christ may dwell in your hearts through faith.*"(Ephesians 3:17)
- *Spiritual fullness.* "*that you may be filled to the measure of all the fullness of God*"(3:19b).
- *Spiritual Adulthood.* "*I write to you, fathers, because you have known him who is from the beginning. I write to you, young men, because you have overcome the evil one. I write to you, dear children, because you have known the Father*"(1 John 2:13).

We Should Have the Same Attitude toward Growth that Paul Has.

That is the meaning of Philippians 3:15. "*All of us who are mature should take such a view of things. And if on some point you think differently, that too God will make clear to you.*" Paul's view of maturity was not perfection. He recognized there would always be room for growth. Paul's view of maturity was not continuing to wallow in sinfulness. He believed that God had brought him to a life of victory and holiness.

We Should Live Up to What We Have Already Attained.

"*Only let us live up to what we have already attained*" (3:16). We should not relax. We should not go backwards. If we have climbed to a level of maturity, we should continue at least at that level. Jesus said, "*From everyone who has been given much, much will be demanded*" Luke 12:48. All of us have been given so much. We will have to give an account of all our wonderful assets one of these days, including the grace of God in our lives.

Maturity in life is normal. If one gets the right balance of food, rest, exercise and exposure to other human beings, he or she will mature normally and naturally. Spiritual maturity is similar but it demands that one be more proactive. One still needs to get spiritual food and spiritual rest and spiritual exercise and must interact with mature believers. However, spiritual maturity takes more initiative than physical maturity. Let us join with Paul and the writer of Hebrews and take that initiative that we might go on to maturity (Hebrews 6:1).

CHAPTER 15

EXAMPLE

(3:17-21)

The Meaning of Being an Example

Paul made what I would consider a startling statement in this paragraph. He wrote, *"Join with others in following my example, brothers, and take note of those who live according to the pattern we gave you"* (3:17). Most Christians are not accustomed to suggesting or even implying that we are worthy of being followed. That might give someone the idea that we think we have arrived and are proud of what we have become. However, Paul was not concerned about giving those impressions. He was a very practical minded person. He recognized that he was living a life that was a good practical model for Christians to follow so he simply encouraged them to follow his example.

"Example" is from the word mimitai from which we get our word "mimic." The word simply means to imitate. So Paul was encouraging the Philippians to imitate his example. Paul was simply saying, "If you live like me, pray like me, worship like me, and witness like me, you will be a successful Christian."

This is not the first time Paul has made such a statement. Note his comments in 1 Corinthians 4:16, *"Therefore I urge you to imitate me."*

How could Paul make what appears to be such an arrogant statement? He answered that question a few chapters later: *"Follow my example, as I follow the example of Christ"* (11:1). Paul could urge people to follow his example because he was following the example of Christ. Paul made a similar statement to the Thessalonians when he said, *"You know how we lived among you for your sake. You became imitators of us and of the Lord"* (1 Thessalonians 1:5-6). Although it might seem strange to us, getting a person to imitate him was one of Paul's discipleship strategies.

The word "pattern" is from *tupos* from which we get our word "type." The word *tupos* was used in the coin making process. A piece of silver or other precious metal would be roughly shaped into the size of a coin. The metal would be placed over a mold and pounded with a hammer until the image of the mold was stamped on the metal. The mold used in the process was called the *tupos*.

Christ was ultimately the mold from which we must all be stamped. His life is a demonstration to us about every aspect of our lives. However, Jesus had gone to heaven. Paul claimed that he was now a mold by which the Philippian Christians could be stamped. Unfortunately, Paul is now gone which means you and I are now the mold to stamp the younger generation of Christians. Would you be happy if the Christians around you became the kind of Christian that you are? Remember, discipleship is ultimately reproducing yourself.

Reasons to Follow Paul's Example

Why could Paul be so bold to encourage the Philippians to imitate him?

Paul was a worthy example.

He had an attitude of compassion. The very fact that Paul would encourage the Philippians to follow his example suggests that he was worthy of being followed. However, there is another hint here. *"For, as*

I have often told you before and now say again even with tears . . ." (3:18). Paul was not a harsh dictator. He was a tenderhearted humble man who could weep as he sought to teach and correct his converts, the Philippians. A man who will weep with compassion is a man who is worthy of being followed.

His citizenship was in heaven. (v. 20a) Paul was a man whose citizenship was in another place. Therefore he lived differently than the ordinary person on the earth.

He was waiting for the coming of Christ. Paul wrote, *"And we eagerly await a Savior from there, the Lord Jesus Christ"* (3:20). Jesus gave several parables about the person who would be waiting and prepared for his second coming. Paul was one of those persons who was anxiously looking forward to the return of Jesus. Because of that, he was a worthy example to be followed.

Here are some questions we must ask ourselves:

- Why should younger Christians follow our example?
- Why should younger missionaries do what we do?
- What things would you like to change before encouraging someone to follow your example?

There were so many poor examples.

Paul wrote,

> "Many live as enemies of the cross of Christ. Their destiny is destruction, their god is their stomach, and their glory is in their shame."
>
> —Phil. 3:18b-19

There are millions of wicked people in the world. Some are found where we work. There are many terrible examples on television. There are even poor examples of people in the church. There are dozens of poor examples of ministry in Nigeria and other parts of Africa. Those who overemphasize the doctrine of prosperity or faith or any other doctrine make it essential that others present a more balanced example. That is why it is so important for you to be a good example.

At a conference, I talked with a missionary who was very discouraged about working in Nigeria. He complained that there was so much selfishness if not downright corruption among the Christians with whom he worked. I tried to encourage him that that was one of the reasons he was there. The missionary not only preaches with his mouth but he preaches with his life. One of our most important jobs as missionaries is to live a humble godly life before our colleagues. It is only as they see good examples that they will know what a real Christian is.

- What kind of example are you to your children?
- What kind of example are you to the other members of your church or your ministry?
- What kind of example are you before new missionaries who come to serve?
- What kind of example are you before your colleagues with whom you work every day?
- What kind of example are you when you go back to your home country? Are you demonstrating what a true missionary should be?

Perhaps one of our most important jobs is being a good example before our colleagues and our students. I recently said in a sermon, "About the only thing more enjoyable for me than preaching a good sermon is to see one of my students preach a good sermon."

There are many things that we Westerners can no longer teach Nigerians. Nigerians are very good evangelists. Nigerians have excellent instincts for worship and prayer. However, God has obviously thought that we could teach something to Nigerians. That is why I and others still serve in Nigeria. Therefore, I would encourage all preachers, teachers and other Christian workers to make a deliberate effort to teach and mentor colleagues to do the job that you are doing.

Peter wrote,

> Live such good lives among the pagans that, though they accuse you of doing wrong, they may see your good deeds and glorify God on the day he visits us.
>
> —1 Peter 2:12

Two related things have impressed me recently in my study of the Bible. The first is the importance of testimony. The most effective thing that we can do is to tell others what we have seen, heard and experienced.

The second thing is this issue of example. We should live such good lives that others can learn about Christ from our lives without us having to say a whole lot about it.

Beauty, the African Gray Parrot

In 1989, we inherited an African Gray parrot whose name is Beauty. The parrot has been a part of our lives ever since. This bird is a natural imitator. She squeaks like doors and brakes. She can make a sound like a car starting. She calls Mary and all my children by name and even speaks Hausa greetings, though with a rather strong American accent. She calls my dogs and even whistles Dixie. I am told that some parrots curse and swear and use God's name in vain. Beauty, though she is a bit obnoxious, does not use any bad language. What is the difference between Beauty and these foul-mouth parrots? Is one more wicked than another? No, a parrot is simply a collector of sounds. They just indiscriminately pick up sounds that they can imitate and repeat them in random order. My parrot even says "Thank you, Lord."

The point is this: If one could tie a parrot to you and that parrot would stay with you long enough to start imitating you, what kind of sounds would it be making? Would they be godly sounds or evil sounds? The real question is: What kind of example are you?

CHAPTER 16

TRANSFORMATION

(3:20-21)

But our citizenship is in heaven. And we eagerly await a Savior from there, the Lord Jesus Christ, who, by the power that enables him to bring everything under his control, will transform our lowly bodies so that they will be like his glorious body.

—Phil. 3:20-21

The key word in this passage is "transform." The particular transformation that this paragraph is talking about is the transformation of our bodies at the resurrection. This is the ultimate transformation.

The Resurrection of Christ

Somewhere near the heart of Christianity is the doctrine of the resurrection of the body. It is the doctrine of the resurrection that sets apart Christianity from all other religions. Here is Paul's summary of the doctrine of the resurrection of Jesus:

If there is no resurrection of the dead, then not even Christ has been raised. And if Christ has not been raised, our preaching is useless and so is your faith. More than that, we are then found to be false witnesses about God, for we have testified about God that he raised

> *Christ from the dead. But he did not raise him if in fact the dead are not raised. For if the dead are not raised, then Christ has not been raised either. And if Christ has not been raised, your faith is futile; you are still in your sins. Then those also who have fallen asleep in Christ are lost. If only for this life we have hope in Christ, we are to be pitied more than all men.*
> —1 Corinthians 15:13-19

The Transformation of Our Bodies

The resurrection of Jesus' body is the foundation stone upon which our own resurrection is based. Paul continues the above statement, *"But Christ has indeed been raised from the dead, the first fruits of those who have fallen asleep"* (15:20). He later describes the transformation in more detail:

> *So will it be with the resurrection of the dead. The body that is sown is perishable, it is raised imperishable; it is sown in dishonor, it is raised in glory; it is sown in weakness, it is raised in power; it is sown a natural body, it is raised a spiritual body.*
> —Phil. 15:42-44

The hope of the Christian is that when this life ends, there will be a future life. And the future life will be better and more glorious than the present life. As Paul says, this old, worn-out, sickness-prone body will be transformed into the kind of body that Jesus had when he appeared to his disciples after the resurrection, a perfect body, prepared for the eternal world.

The Transformation of Our Lives

However, there is even better news. Our transformation does not begin at the resurrection. It begins much earlier.

When God made man and woman, he made them in his own image. We do not know all that that means but it certainly means that there were some similarities between God and the humans he created. When the man and woman turned their back on God and fell into sin, they fell into disfavor with God and lost some of that image. Ever since that time, God has been working to see the human race transformed back into His image. That is why Jesus came into this world—to change us and put us back in fellowship and relationship with God.

Note this process: The first practical step is when we are regenerated—when we personally commit ourselves to Christ. God brings a great transformation process in our lives at that time.

"Therefore, if anyone is in Christ, he is a new creation; the old has gone, the new has come!" (2 Corinthians 5:17). However, we are not as changed as we should be or will be. Our relationship with God has changed. We are now a child not an enemy. Our spirit has changed. We are now able to interact with God. However, like the change in a new baby, the process of change continues. Paul wrote,

> *Therefore, I urge you, brothers, in view of God's mercy, to offer your bodies as living sacrifices, holy and pleasing to God—this is your spiritual act of worship. Do not conform any longer to the pattern of this world, but be transformed by the renewing of your mind. Then you will be able to test and approve what God's will is—his good, pleasing and perfect will.*
> —Romans 12:1-2

The Greek word "transformed" in this verse is *metamorphoo* from which we get "metamorphosis." This is a word from biology that describes the gradual change that takes place in certain living creatures. For example an egg changes to a worm and then worm changed into a cocoon and then the cocoon eventually produces a butterfly. Therefore, what this passage suggests to us is that all through our lives, we are continually being changed into the image of Christ.

In 2 Corinthians 3:18, Paul wrote,

> *And we, who with unveiled faces all reflect the Lord's glory, are being transformed into his likeness with ever-increasing glory, which comes from the Lord, who is the Spirit.*

This verse says that we are continually being transformed into his likeness. This passage provides us with another interesting word picture. Our faces are like mirrors that reflect what is inside us. In this case, our faces are reflecting the glory of God. When someone looks at us, they see the glory of God reflected as in a mirror. It is like we are a mirror which is held at a 45-degree angle. As God shines down from above, his glory is reflected out at a right angle from us. In the immediate preceding context, Paul uses the illustration of Moses who, when he came into the presence of God, had to put a veil over his face because it was so radiant. However, he says that we do not and should not put a veil over our faces. Our faces should continue to reflect the glory of God.

A mirror should not draw attention to itself. It should simply reflect what is in front of it. A mirror does not usually draw attention to itself. Two things will draw attention to a mirror.

- If it is dirty, one will notice the mirror. If the mirror has been splashed with soapy water or has something else on it that is not supposed to be there, it will draw attention to itself.
- If it is distorted, one will notice the mirror. Some mirrors are warped and thus give a distorted image of whatever they reflect.

The point should be obvious. We should not be drawing attention to ourselves. However, we will certainly draw attention to ourselves if we have the dirt of sin in our lives. In addition, we will also draw attention to ourselves if we have become distorted through becoming out of balance.

We get a glimpse of the glory of Jesus at the transfiguration when it appears that God rolled back the curtain of heaven and allowed the disciples to get a little glimpse of the true glory of Jesus.

> *After six days Jesus took with him Peter, James and John the brother of James, and led them up a high mountain by themselves. There he was transfigured before them. His face shone like the sun, and his clothes became as white as the light.*
> —Matthew 17:1-2

Peter and the other disciples had never seen anything like this so they struggled to find the right human words to describe the beauty and purity and holiness of what they had experienced.

As Christian believers, we are now reflecting the glory, beauty and purity of God. However, we should continue to reflect God's glory in a greater and greater way throughout our lives. As I indicated earlier, there is a day coming in the future when we will receive glorified bodies and our ability to reflect the glory of God will then be complete.

One of the things that I would like to add to this discussion goes beyond what Paul mentions in this passage. It is something that the Reformed tradition has felt strongly about and, in fact, has led at least the Protestant world in understanding. I speak of not just the transformation of the individual but the transformation of society.

The Transformation of Society

A careful reading of the Bible will confirm that God is not just interesting in the transformation of individuals. God wants to see enough individuals transformed that this transforms the society.

The study of "revival" throughout church history is a fascinating topic. I am not sure that I know a good formal definition of revival. However, it is my understanding that revivals have taken place when

God has moved in such a way that the whole community or the whole society has changed.

Whether it is supernatural and happens in a short time or whether it is a result of teaching and preaching and discipleship, we should not be satisfied until we see righteousness and justice entrenched in the society. When we see such things happen we are seeing God's will being done on earth as it is in heaven.

Summary

God is a God of transformation. We should make sure that we are not only being transformed but that we are being agents of transformation as well.

CHAPTER 17

RECONCILIATION

(4:2-3)

There were two ladies in the Philippian church who had had a sharp disagreement with one another. We know nothing about what had caused the problem. Maybe it was a disagreement over what to name the women's fellowship. Maybe it was a disagreement over who would teach the Sunday School class. Maybe it was a disagreement over who would play the musical instrument for the church choir.

There are two fairly obvious conclusions about the problem: First, it was a problem that the whole church knew about and was influencing the whole church. Second, it was a solvable problem—something that could be worked out.

Paul wrote, *"I plead with Euodia and I plead with Syntyche to agree with each other in the Lord"* (4:2). Paul recognized that disunity is one of the biggest enemies of the church. Therefore, he addressed the issue of reconciliation of these ladies in a public letter to the church.

What Paul was trying to do was engage in the ministry of reconciliation. It is one of the most important ministries in which the Christian or church worker can be involved.

We have talked about disunity earlier. Now we must talk about the solution for disunity. It is almost inevitable that problems and disagreements are going to develop between people who feel strongly about things. Disagreements can produce grief and heartache. However, there is no greater ministry than the ministry of reconciliation.

The first step in reconciling two estranged believers is hinted at in this very verse. Paul pleaded with the two ladies *"to agree with each other **in the Lord**."* This statement suggests that these ladies should agree together because they are both *"in the Lord."* They were both serving Jesus Christ. They were both sisters in Christ. They were both members of the body of Christ. They were both depending up the sacrifice of Jesus to provide forgiveness of their sins and salvation. Therefore, since they were both in Christ, they should make effort to restore peace and harmony.

When we take our eyes off from Jesus Christ and start focusing on the peripheral issues of our faith, our differences become magnified. However, when we focus on Jesus and all that he has done for us and to us, our differences fade into the background. We used to sing an old song that says,

> *Turn your eyes upon Jesus.*
> *Look full into his wonderful face.*
> *And the things of earth will grow strangely dim*
> *In the light of his glory and grace.*

Jesus was concerned about unity. He recognized that there are always going to be times when people disagree, sometimes strongly. Therefore, he gave us some guidelines for reconciling with those who are estranged. Note these two teachings from Jesus.

> *Therefore, if you are offering your gift at the altar and there remember that your brother has something against you, leave your*

> *gift there in front of the altar. First go and be reconciled to your brother; then come and offer your gift*
> —Matthew 5:23-24

There are four specific points of application:

Solve problems quickly.

This passage describes a person going to the temple either to make a sacrifice or perhaps to give a gift as part of his worship to God. The priest goes to the altar and is about to slaughter the animal and make the sacrifice. All of a sudden the worshipper remembers a problem that has developed between him and another person. His mind has not been purged of the offense that was committed against the friend or the barrier that has come up between them. Jesus said that he was to leave the gift at the altar and to go and be reconciled to the brother before coming and trying to worship God.

The point that Jesus is making is that as soon as you become aware that there is a problem between you and another person, that is the time to solve the problem. The only fuel that problems need to spread is time. The best way to escalate a disagreement with a friend is delay. Therefore, the best thing we can do to stop a problem is deal with it quickly.

Solve problems directly.

Jesus also said:

> *If your brother sins against you, go and show him his fault, just between the two of you. If he listens to you, you have won your brother over. But if he will not listen, take one or two others along, so that every matter may be established by the testimony of two or three witnesses. If he refuses to listen to them, tell it to the church; and if he*

> *refuses to listen even to the church, treat him as you would a pagan or a tax collector*
> —Matthew 18:15-17

The point is simple: The best way to solve a problem is to go directly to the person involved and try to resolve it.

That is not always possible. Some cultures are much more indirect in solving problems. Sometimes the person involved may not agree to see you. However, inasmuch as possible, we should attempt to solve our problems as directly as possible.

Solve problems openly.

Note that Paul did not send a private letter to certain persons in the church and ask them to help resolve this problem. It was obvious that the problem had become public. Therefore, Paul wanted the whole church to know that the problem should be resolved. Note also this comment from 1 Corinthians 1:10-11,

> *I appeal to you, brothers, in the name of our Lord Jesus Christ, that all of you agree with one another so that there may be no divisions among you and that you may be perfectly united in mind and thought. My brothers, some from Chloe's household have informed me that there are quarrels among you.*

On this occasion Paul appealed in an open letter to the church at Corinth to heal a division.

Note also that Paul revealed his source of information. The information came from Chloe's household. Obviously private problems should be solved privately. There is no justification to drag out personal disputes into the public. However, the Apostle Paul demonstrated here that whenever a problem has reached the public, it should be handled in a direct public manner.

Solve problems specifically.
Note Paul's comments in 1 Corinthians 1:12,

> What I mean is this: One of you says, "I follow Paul"; another, "I follow Apollos"; another, "I follow Cephas"; still another, "I follow Christ."

Paul identified the specific problem and sought to solve the problem very specifically.

When solving problems of division or estrangement we have two tendencies. The first is to generalize the problem. When attempting to reconcile differences we tend to say to our adversary, "Well, there seems to be something between us . . . and if I have done anything wrong . . ."

There may be situations in which we do not know the specific problem. However, most of the time, if there is a conflict with another person, we know what it is. Be specific about your own fault. If you do not know of a specific problem, you can usually confess that you have been angry and unforgiving and you have been guilty of gossip and other things.

The second tendency is to blame the other person either directly or indirectly. We sometimes begin our confession, "Now, I know I made some mistakes but you . . ." It is important instead to focus on our own faults and failures and allow the Holy Spirit to convict others of their failures. It is amazing once you have confessed your faults, how quickly the others will confess their faults and how anxious they will be for reconciliation.

Reconciliation with a Messenger
Some years ago, one of my colleagues at the university casually mentioned, "You know Moses, the messenger in our department, really hates you." That got my attention. I do not like for people to hate me. I knew the issue. I had coordinated a certain programme and the people

in the department put a lot of pressure on me to "share" some of the proceeds with them. However, this messenger had done no extra work for the programme so I refused to give him or anyone else unconnected with the project any extra money. Unfortunately, he took the case personally and apparently started saying negative things about me.

The next day I went to him and called him over to a quiet place. He greeted me quite warmly. I said, "Moses, I have something I want to say to you. I remember some time ago you wanted me to share some of the money with you from the DCS programme. I have thought about that and I want you to know that I made a big mistake. I did not handle the situation correctly. I really did not have the authority to give you any of that money. However, instead of explaining the issue to you, I simply ignored your request. That was wrong. You had a right to know why I could not give you any of the money. I am sorry that I failed to properly inform you and I am asking you to forgive me. And now I want to give you a little personal gift to just let you know that I am sorry that I did not treat you properly."

Moses started shaking his head, "No, sir. You do not need to give me anything. The fact that you, a big man in the university, would come to me and say 'sorry' is all the blessing I could ever want." I can assure you that I never had any more problems from Moses and never heard any more negative reports. From then on, in fact, he would go out of his way to do anything for me. My apology did not cost me much. However, it paid big dividends.

We should not allow un-reconciled differences to exist among us. If there is a difference between you and a friend or one of your leaders or a family member, you should try to repair it. Do not wait for the other person to come to you. You take the initiative and confess your faults.

Reconciliation of Two Missionary Organizations

In 1975, Mary and I joined a team doing evangelistic work in Alaska. The following summer we went back to Alaska to work among Indians along the Yukon River. Later I was asked by an Alaskan mission organization to serve on their board of directors. In my acceptance letter I stated that there was one thing I would like to see done differently if I were to serve on the board. About five years before, a serious disagreement arose between the founder and some of the missionaries, which led to a nasty separation. Some missionaries pulled out and started their own parallel organization doing much the same kind of ministry. I knew that there was a lot of bitterness between the two groups.

At our first board meeting I made a little speech, that on the strength of Jesus' teachings about reconciliation, before we could really serve God freely and have God's blessing and joy with us, we needed to be reconciled with the leaders of the other organization. I was a little surprised at how eager the board was to do this. There was really no opposition. It seemed that they had hesitated and allowed these things to fester simply because no one had challenged them to be reconciled.

We wrote a very straightforward letter stating that we had been guilty of gossip and criticism toward the other organization and their individual members and we asked them to forgive us for these sins against them and against God. We made an appointment to meet with the chairman of the other organization. Our entire board went to the meeting. The meeting was very tense at first but our chairman said, "Brother, we have something that we want to say to you. We have written it down so that we will say everything exactly as we feel it and we have come as the entire board to let you know we are unanimous in our feelings about this." He then read the letter:"

> Without reopening old wounds, we would like to simply say that we are indeed sorry that we were so insensitive to your needs and convictions back then. Time has a tendency to blur things and it is really difficult to remember all of the issues and the various things that were said or left unsaid. In reviewing these things, we have felt convicted that we did not handle things properly back then. Certainly there were times when we were not always kind and considerate as Christians should be. Also, we tended to have a divisive spirit—seeking to get our own way rather than trying to maintain harmony in the organization. We were also guilty of criticizing those who did not agree with our positions. All in all, we know that we were a great disappointment to God in the way we did things. All of these things now bring to us a deep sense of sorrow and shame . . . We would like to say that we are sincerely sorry for the hurt and grief that we have caused each of you, your family members, and your organization. We would also like to ask you to forgive us for our lack of sensitivity to your convictions, our unkind and critical attitudes, and our failure to solve our problems according to God's blueprint.

The other chairman stood up, and for some time, struggled to say anything. He finally said they had been guilty of everything we had mentioned and he asked us if we would forgive him personally as well as all those who had been a part of his organization. The two chairmen then fell into each other's arms and they wept for the next 15 minutes. One could almost feel the restoration taking place. We finally left that meeting with a feeling of cleansing and wholeness and happiness. You cannot imagine the joy we experienced after that wonderful meeting.

If, like Paul urged Euodia and Syntyche, you *"agree with each other,"* I assure you that you will experience more joy than you could ever have imagined. Let us not allow petty differences to divide us and steal our joy. Let us make every effort to make sure that as much as lies within us, we are at peace with all (Hebrews 12:14).

CHAPTER 18

PRAYER

(4:4-7)

Rejoice in the Lord always. I will say it again: Rejoice! Let your gentleness be evident to all. The Lord is near. Do not be anxious about anything, but in everything, by prayer and petition, with thanksgiving, present your requests to God. And the peace of God, which transcends all understanding, will guard your hearts and your minds in Christ Jesus.

Paul began this paragraph by encouraging the Philippians to rejoice again. The word "joy" or "rejoice" is found in this little book 14 times in four short chapters.

A second theme Paul stressed in this paragraph was prayer. He urged the Philippians not to be anxious but *"in everything, by prayer and petition, with thanksgiving, present your request to God"* (4:6) One of the greatest privileges that the Christian has is the joy of prayer, to actually talk to the God of the universe.

Some of you have personally seen or shaken hands or perhaps even met and chatted with the head of state of your country. You can remember the date, the place, the circumstances, what you said and what he or she said. However, do you realize that we have the privilege of talking not to the president of the Federal Republic of Nigeria but to the God of the universe?

One of the blessings of prayer is being able to take all our problems and difficulties to one who can do something about them. One of the joys I have in prayer is to pray for others. I have a fairly long prayer list of people and organizations I pray for regularly. To pray for these people is a special privilege.

Because prayer is such a special privilege, I want to focus a bit more on it. There are many kinds of prayers in the Bible. We will take a look at some of them.

Genuine and Hypocritical Prayers

Jesus acknowledged that not all prayers are sincere. He said,

> *And when you pray, do not be like the hypocrites, for they love to pray standing in the synagogues and on the street corners to be seen by men. I tell you the truth, they have received their reward in full. But when you pray, go into your room, close the door and pray to your Father, who is unseen. Then your Father, who sees what is done in secret, will reward you.*
>
> —Matthew 6:5-6

This statement suggests that some people, like the Pharisees, pray insincerely (Isaiah 1:15; Jeremiah 7:16). They pray publically and they pray dramatically in such a way to been seen and respected by others. Jesus declared that such hypocritical prayers produce the only reward they will get—the false feeling of importance when they perceive other people are admiring them.

To avoid such hypocritical prayers, Jesus urged the sincere person to pray secretly and quietly. It is this kind of genuine prayer that will unlock the heart of God and cause him to answer the prayer.

Public and Private Prayers

The previous passage suggests that the best way to pray is in private. Daniel practiced such private prayers in the Old Testament (Daniel 6:10). Jesus himself illustrates the importance of private praying. Immediately after the amazing miracle of feeding the 5000, we read, *"After he had dismissed them, he went up on a mountainside by himself to pray"* (Matthew 14:23). In fact, Luke 5:16 says, *"Jesus often withdrew to lonely places and prayed."*

However, as the wise man said, there is a time and place for everything (Ecclesiastes 3:1), including public prayers. There are many public prayers recording in the Bible:

- Solomon prayed publically when he dedicated the Temple (1 Kings 8:23-61; 2 Chronicles 6:14-42)
- Elijah prayed publically when he challenged the prophets of Baal (1 Kings 18:36-37).
- Ezra prayed publically at the altar when hearing of the sins of the Israelite leaders (Ezra 9:6-15).
- The Levites at the direction of Nehemiah prayed a long prayer of confession and commitment after Ezra read the Law (Nehemiah 9:5-38).
- Jesus prayed publically for his disciples during his last night on the earth (John 17:1-26).

Though our relationship with God is primarily a private one, there our times, when public prayer is appropriate and important.

Long and Short Prayers

When I was a young Christian, the church in which I was raised believed that the average Christian should pray an hour a day. Korean Christians are known for the long periods of time they spend in prayer.

However, there is no prescribed length of our prayers. There were some very long prayers and some very short prayers in the Bible.

We are told that Jesus went into a mountain and prayed all night (Luke 6:12). In addition, immediately after his baptism, Jesus went into the wilderness where he spent 40 days fasting (Matthew 4:2; Mark 1:13; Luke 4:2). We are not told specifically that Jesus was praying but fasting is nearly always linked with praying.

On the other hand, the prayer that Elijah prayed in contest with the prophets of Baal was only 60 words long in the NIV (1 Kings 18:36-37; 41 words in Hebrew) and yet it was one of the most powerful prayers recorded in the Bible.

Oral and Written Prayers

Most of the prayers that are recorded in the Bible were prayed orally and later written down. Therefore, we tend to think that the default type of praying is oral praying. However, there are also many written prayers found in the Bible as well.

Many of the psalms contain prayers of many kinds:

- *Prayer of Repentance: Have mercy on me, O God, according to your unfailing love; according to your great compassion blot out my transgressions. Wash away all my iniquity and cleanse me from my sin. For I know my transgressions, and my sin is always before me. Against you, you only, have I sinned and done what is evil in your sight, so that you are proved right when you speak and justified when you judge* (51:1-4).
- *Prayer for Protection: But I pray to you, O Lord, in the time of your favor; in your great love, O God, answer me with your sure salvation. Rescue me from the mire, do not let me sink; deliver me from those who hate me, from the deep waters. Do not let the floodwaters engulf me or the depths swallow me up or the pit close its mouth over me. Answer me, O Lord, out of the goodness of your love; in your great mercy turn to me* (69:13-16).

- *Prayer of Complaint: I say to God my Rock, Why have you forgotten me? Why must I go about mourning, oppressed by the enemy?" My bones suffer mortal agony as my foes taunt me, saying to me all day long, "Where is your God?" Why are you downcast, O my soul? Why so disturbed within me? Put your hope in God, for I will yet praise him, my Savior and my God* (42:9-11).

There are also wonderful written prayers in the New Testament. In fact some of the most profound appeals for discipleship and holiness are found in the written prayers of the New Testament.

- *Ephesians 3:15-19, For this reason I kneel before the Father, from whom his whole family in heaven and on earth derives its name. I pray that out of his glorious riches he may strengthen you with power through his Spirit in your inner being, so that Christ may dwell in your hearts through faith. And I pray that you, being rooted and established in love, may have power, together with all the saints, to grasp how wide and long and high and deep is the love of Christ, and to know this love that surpasses knowledge—that you may be filled to the measure of all the fullness of God.*
- *1 Thessalonians 5:23-24, May God himself, the God of peace, sanctify you through and through. May your whole spirit, soul and body be kept blameless at the coming of our Lord Jesus Christ. The one who calls you is faithful and he will do it.*

These prayers describe a level of holiness and spiritual maturity that few people every really achieve. I am glad that Paul believed in writing out his prayers.

One of the best things that I have learned in my spiritual growth is the importance of writing. I have been faithful to write out my sermons and lectures for the past 35 years. That has been a great blessing to me because many of those have found their way into books and have been able to bless people other than the original audience. However, perhaps even more important is the lesson that I have learned about writing out the reflections and meditations in my daily quiet time.

In October of 1998, I decided that I wanted to read through the Bible very carefully and take a lot of notes. These notes consist of anything that I think of during the time I am meditating, including observations, questions, cross references, illustrations, applications, summaries, outlines, parallel translations and, of course, prayers. I have taken all of these notes on my computer. During this 15 year project, I have typed out over 5700 pages of devotional notes including thousands of prayers. There is something about writing out prayers that helps you to think through and articulate them better. Praying on paper is something that I believe every believer could benefit from.

Vocal and Silent Prayers

Almost all of the prayers in the Bible are vocal or written to be vocalized. However, is it possible to pray when you do not actually vocalize words?

The person who best illustrates this is Hannah. She would go to the tabernacle regularly and pray that God would give her a child. On one particular visit, we read this record: *"Hannah was praying in her heart, and her lips were moving but her voice was not heard"* (1 Samuel 1:12). This silent prayer proved to be a very powerful one because within one year, God had answered Hannah's prayer and she had received her first-born child.

Our faith teaches us that God is omniscient which means that he knows everything, even the thoughts that we have. The Psalmist declared *"The Lord knows the thoughts of man"* (94:11) and David himself stated to his son Solomon that the Lord not only knew the thoughts but *"understands every motive behind the thoughts"* (1 Chronicles 28:9). If

God knows the thoughts and we are able to formulate prayers in our thoughts, then God understands those prayers as well.

Adoration and Complaint Prayers

One of the key parts of prayer is adoration and worship. This is basically speaking to God and recognizing and attributing to him the attributes and moral qualities that he possesses. Note these examples:

- Moses prayed (in a song): *Who among the gods is like you, O Lord? Who is like you—majestic in holiness, awesome in glory, working wonders?* (Exodus 15:11).
- David prayed: *Praise be to you, O Lord, God of our father Israel, from everlasting to everlasting. Yours, O Lord, is the greatness and the power and the glory and the majesty and the splendor, for everything in heaven and earth is yours. Yours, O Lord, is the kingdom; you are exalted as head over all. Wealth and honor come from you; you are the ruler of all things. In your hands are strength and power to exalt and give strength to all* (1 Chronicles 29:10-12).
- The 24 elders in Revelation prayed: *You are worthy, our Lord and God, to receive glory and honor and power, for you created all things, and by your will they were created and have their being* (4:11).

However, not everyone prayed such prayers of adoration to God. There are some prayers that contain serious complaints. Note these examples:

- Job challenged God: *Do not condemn me, but tell me what charges you have against me. Does it please you to oppress me, to spurn the work of your hands, while you smile on the schemes of the wicked? Do you have eyes of flesh? Do you see as a mortal sees? Are your days like those of a mortal or your years like those of a man, that you must search out my faults and probe after my sin—though you know that I am not guilty and that no one can rescue me from your hand?* (10:2-7).

- *Habakkuk complained to God, How long, O Lord, must I call for help, but you do not listen? Or cry out to you, "Violence!" but you do not save? Why do you make me look at injustice? Why do you tolerate wrong? Destruction and violence are before me; there is strife, and conflict abounds. Therefore the law is paralyzed, and justice never prevails. The wicked hem in the righteous, so that justice is perverted* (1:2-4).
- *Jeremiah questioned God: You are always righteous, O Lord, when I bring a case before you. Yet I would speak with you about your justice: Why does the way of the wicked prosper? Why do all the faithless live at ease?* (12:1).

To be honest, these prayers scare me a little. How can a mortal man question God Almighty? Amazingly, God did not seem to get angry at these complaints. In fact, God seemed to welcome the honest questions from his faithful servants. This suggests something about prayer that we do not think about enough. Perhaps prayer is more about the communication with God than the requests that are made to God. God is pleased when his servants pray to him, even when they do not understand something.

Regular and Emergency Prayers

There has traditionally been tension between scheduling prayers as a routine exercise and praying only whenever there is a big need. However, both were common things in the Bible.

There were regular times of prayer. Acts 3:1 introduces us to the story about Peter healing a blind man at the Beautiful Gate of the Temple: "*One day Peter and John were going up to the temple at the time of prayer —at three in the afternoon.*" This passage tells us that this was a regular daily time of prayer. Apparently the early Christians continued praying daily in the Temple at the normal times for Jewish sacrifices and prayer which were 9 AM, 12 noon and 3 PM.

There were regular places of prayer. The previous passage tells us that the early Christians were quite predictable in their prayers. They went to the Temple daily to pray.

There was a regular pattern of prayer. Jesus taught his disciples a sample prayer which Christians have followed from that day to this:

> Our Father in heaven, hallowed be your name, your kingdom come, your will be done on earth as it is in heaven. Give us today our daily bread. Forgive us our debts, as we also have forgiven our debtors. And lead us not into temptation, but deliver us from the evil one.
> —Matthew 6:9-13

All of these demonstrate that prayer could become quite regular and routine.

There is nothing wrong with having a regular time of prayer. Good habits are good for us. However, we should not limit our prayers to just memorized prayers or prayers at a certain time and place. God is concerned about all of our activities. Therefore, we should be prepared to pray emergency prayers when there is a need.

When Nehemiah learned of the terrible conditions of the city of Jerusalem, he thought and prayed about this. Eventually the king detected something was troubling him and asked him about it. Nehemiah replied that he could not help from feeling unhappy since the city of his fathers was in ruins. Nehemiah then records the next exchange.

> The king said to me, "What is it you want?" Then I prayed to the God of heaven, and I answered the king, "If it pleases the king and if your servant has found favor in his sight, let him send me to the city in Judah where my fathers are buried so that I can rebuild it."
> —Phil. 2:4-5

Nehemiah probably did not pray out loud but he prayed an emergency prayer to God for guidance and he then made his request to the king.

There are other emergency prayers in the Bible. Note these emergency prayers just in the Book of Acts:

- The Church prayed for God's wisdom immediately after Peter and John were released from prison the first time (4:23-30; See also 12:5, 12).
- Stephen prayed that the Lord would receive his spirit when he was being stoned to death and also that his persecutors would be forgiven (7:59-60).
- Peter prayed for Dorcas when he arrived in Joppa and found she had died (9:40-41).
- Paul and Silas were praying and singing hymns at midnight in the Philippians jail (16:25).
- Paul prayed for Publius' father on the island of Malta after he had been shipwrecked there (28:8).

Everyone has experienced emergency or dangerous times in which we have been forced to send up emergency prayers to the Lord. I will conclude this section by sharing a prayer meeting I once observed in a difficult situation.

Prayers During a Crisis

The city of Jos where I live experienced a very serious political/ethnic/religious clash starting on 7 September 2001. We had about 150 fearful people show up at our house, seeking shelter from the roving gangs who were burning and killing. We began feeding them and at least 70 of them spent the night in our house each night for several nights. It was a very emotional experience. I was up and down a good bit in the night checking on our visitors and also checking with my neighbors who had organized themselves to provide some protection for our community.

All during this crisis, I kept a detailed journal of events. Whenever there was a little break in the activities, I would sit down at my computer and write what I had just seen and experienced. The following is a page from my journal the morning of 9 September 2001. As you will see, I was trying to describe the things that I was seeing and hearing at that moment so the organization reflects the events as they were unfolding. I think these notes will give some insight into Paul's statements that we should do everything with prayers and petitions especially in difficult or emergency situations:

> I came back downstairs and as I was walking down the steps, I heard noise. It was the sound of women singing quietly. At the present time (5:34 AM), they are still singing. However, they are singing much more loudly and vigorously now. They began by singing *"Good morning Jesus"* and similar morning choruses. They sang *Mun gode Allah*. They are now singing an Igbo chorus. One of the ladies is leading and the others are following as they normally do in church. Next chorus: *We have come again. Holy Ghost, we have come again, Holy Ghost, come and take control.* It is amazing that many of those ladies lost all of their possessions yesterday except what they could carry with them. Yet this morning they are singing praises to God with enthusiasm. Next chorus: another Hausa chorus; (long burst of gunfire in the distance). Some lady is now leading in prayer and at the appropriate places all of the ladies will say "Amen." All of the ladies are praying out loud at one time, which is very common here. I cannot hear everything but I continue to hear the phrase "Thank God for . . ." "Thank God for . . ." If I had just lost all my possessions and my husband and older sons had been gone for twenty four hours and I did not know whether they were dead or alive, would I have that same spirit of thanksgiving and praise? Now the chorus: *Thank you, Jesus.* After a period of

prayer: New chorus: *Oh, the blood of Jesus. Oh the blood of Jesus, Oh the blood of Jesus, that washes white as snow.*

It is interesting that yesterday, I could not really detect any of the ladies who were taking charge of things except for one lady who was working in the kitchen. However, some lady is definitely taking charge of the prayer meeting. And there is no longer any attempt at restraint. They are singing seriously. (Several more bursts of gunfire in the distance). They are singing a Hausa chorus right now which I don't know. Here is another chorus: *When we come into your presence, I am so happy. When I come into your presence, I am so glad. In your presence, there is anointing with the Spirit all around us, with your presence there is anointing, Praise the Lord.* Another prayer, "We want to thank you . . ." This was another long passionate prayer in which the lady thanked the Lord for many things and then, in the prayer, encouraged everyone to call on the name of the Lord. She said, "Our reverends have reminded us to call on the name of the Lord when we are in trouble. We are in trouble so we are calling on your name." She asked for protection from their enemies for everyone that is in the north, whether they are from the east or west or the north. She then urged everyone to pray again and so they prayed loudly for the next several minutes.

It is now 5:54 and we are just now beginning to see the first hints of light in the east. Thank you, Lord, for the sunlight of another day. There is some kind of big bird that is making a lot of noise outside right now. The roosters are crowing and so there are very positive morning sounds, mixed with gunfire.

One of the ladies is exhorting the women now. She talked to them briefly about death: that Jesus would be with them in death if God called them to die. She then urged them to pray for their children, their husbands or wives, for their country and for themselves. They then went into another season of rather moderately loud praying. While they are praying, one lady is singing quietly, "*I surrender all.*" The lady is exhorting again. She encouraged them to surrender everything to Jesus. Now everyone is singing the chorus "*I surrender all. All to Jesus blessed Savior, I surrender all.*" The lady is now leading in prayer again. "We surrender our lives; we surrender our properties to you. From this morning we surrender; our leaders, we surrender; our bodies, we surrender. We pray, O God that you will guide and protect us. Let us put our trust in you, O God." Another minute of serious praying. The lady then exhorting them to thank the Lord for the family who had taken them in and urged them to pray for us and ask God to bless us in many ways. There followed a serious volume of prayer. I type this with tears running down my cheeks—to think that these people are thinking of us, with our abundance when they have suffered so much. Another person was called on to pray who has an older voice. She is vigorously praying for us who welcomed them. She asked that the Lord would give us the mind of peace and love. Because it is not easy to feed people like we have, she prayed God would supply all our needs.

The original lady is now exhorting them that they have to take authority over the devil and the enemy and pray that the Lord will cancel all the plans of the enemy. She is urging them to pray that any weapon that people take up against them will not prosper. The group is now praying very loudly. (It is now 6:10 and good daylight.)

What an absolutely incredible experience—to sit here in my office and hear these people pray so earnestly—who have just lost so much and who still face great danger and uncertainty. The leader is praying again. She is praying about the time that the disciples were in the boat and Jesus was sleeping but when he awoke, the wind had to stop blowing. She says, "Jesus, Papa, we are reminding you that no weapon formed against us will prosper. What is happening to us is not the plan of God. Any of our people that they are attacking right now, we pray that you would stop them. We come against them with the Word of God. We come against them in the name of Jesus. We come against them with the Holy Ghost. We bless your holy name. All that we have prayed, we pray with the blood of Jesus. All of our leaders, we cover with the blood of Jesus. All the Muslims, we pray that they will be confused. We thank you for the way you have kept us. We thank you from the east and from the west. Papa, guide us and protect us. When they are at our front, be at our front; when they are at our back, be at our back. In Jesus mighty name." And everyone quotes together, "And surely goodness and mercy shall follow us all the days of our lives and we shall dwell in the house of the Lord forever. May the grace of our Lord Jesus Christ, the love of God and the fellowship of the Holy Spirit be with us."

I pray the Lord will teach me to pray with such calmness and sincerity and passion if I ever have to face such an emergency again.

Prayer is one of the most important tools you as followers of Jesus have. Make sure that *"in everything, by prayer and petition, with thanksgiving,* (you) *present your requests to God."* If you do that I believe *"the peace of God, which transcends all understanding, will guard your hearts and your minds in Christ Jesus."* Phil. 4:6-7

CHAPTER 19

OPTIMISM

(4:8-9)

Finally, brothers, whatever is true, whatever is noble, whatever is right, whatever is pure, whatever is lovely, whatever is admirable—if anything is excellent or praiseworthy—think about such things.
—Phil. 4:8

Of all the verses in the Bible, I think that Philippians 4:8 is perhaps the most convicting. At least, it is convicting for me. To be honest many of the temptations of the world are no problem for me. I have not stolen anything for at least 40 years and have never really been seriously tempted to steal during that time. I have no problem in refraining from cursing and using vulgar language. God has also been gracious in helping me to tell the truth.

However, Paul elevates the standard of the Christian life above just those external things to the thoughts in our mind. Jesus said, *"But I tell you that anyone who looks at a woman lustfully has already committed adultery with her in his heart"* (Matthew 5:28). This suggests to us that it is not only our outward behaviour that is important to God. Our thought life is equally if not more important. God does not want us thinking evil thoughts.

However, Paul raises the standard even higher. He stated that it is not good enough just to refrain from evil thoughts. We should fill our minds with positive things. When our minds are not actively engaged in our work or some other essential duty, we should try to concentrate on good and positive and wholesome things. Paul gave a description of the types of things about which we should be thinking:

- *True.* There is nothing unique about truth. It is simply what has happened and what is. It is the opposite of deception and lying. God expects us to fill our mind with truth. If our minds are continually filled with truth, it is easier to spot error and untruth.
- *Noble.* The word "noble" refers to those things that are high and lofty, qualities of high moral character such as honor, generosity and courage. The words dignity and majestic are associated with the word noble.
- *Right.* This refers to righteousness and justice. God expects us to think about things that are just. Rather than thinking about ways to get around the rules and regulations, we need to focus on doing what is right.
- *Pure.* This obviously refers to things that are morally pure. God does not want us to think about the things of the gutter. He does not want us to think about things that will stain our conscience and our memory.
- *Lovely.* This refers to things that are pleasing to the eyes, things like beautiful flowers and beautiful scenery. God is pleased with those who draw beautiful pictures because they help to fulfill the Scripture that encourages us to think on beautiful things. God is happy with the choir when it produces beautiful music.
- *Admirable.* This refers to things you respect. Most of the time we use the word "admire" when talking about people. We do not admire

beautiful houses. We admire the handiwork of the craftsman who built them. This ultimately refers to good character qualities.
- *Excellent.* This refers to people who do exceptional work. God is a God of excellence who has created the universe according to that standard. He expects us to think about and strive for excellence in our work.
- *Praiseworthy.* This is almost a summary of all the other words. If something is true and pure and lovely, it is worthy of praise. Anything worthy of praise is worth thinking about and is what should fill our minds.

This list of words provides a great challenge for us. If we are going to fulfill the Scripture in thinking about these types of things, it is going to require great effort on our part. Here are three specific applications based on this simple truth, which should apply equally to all believers.

We Must Think about Pure Things.

When we put all of these words and phrases together, we see that Paul was urging the Philippians to have a morally pure thought life. We should think about things that are pure and right and holy. We must refuse to think about things that are unrighteous, impure and unholy.

This suggests we must guard our minds by guarding our ears and eyes and friendships so we do not allow impure and unholy things to become part of our thinking. The psalmist wrote "I will set before my eyes no vile thing" (101:3). Making that commitment helps one to keep pure thoughts.

Jesus said if a man looks upon a woman to lust after her, he has committed adultery with her in his heart. This kind of sin can easily be secret. No one may know anything about that sinful thought. However, the lingering look of the eye encourages mental adultery. Job wrote, *"I made a covenant with my eyes not to look lustfully at a girl"* (31:1).

The way we think about things is by entering that data primarily through our eyes and ears. We think about things that we see and hear and read. Therefore, we must be careful that we look at and read and listen to things that are positive and holy and not negative and sinful.

Our world is filled with much evil. There are times when we cannot avoid seeing and hearing and thinking about evil. However, we control most of the activities of our lives. Therefore, we must make a deliberate decision not to allow our minds to be filled with impure thoughts. If we do, we will soon begin thinking the same thoughts on our own.

When I gave my life to Christ as a teenager, God so cleaned up my mouth that I would go weeks without even thinking about a curse word. Later, however, I started working around construction workers and many of these people have very dirty and vulgar mouths. After being around this crowd for some time, I noticed that curse words would pop into my mind at various times when it would be "appropriate" to use such a word if I were still using that language. That taught me something important about my associations. They affect the way I think.

I cannot always help being around certain kinds of people and hearing bad language on the job. However, I can help what kinds of friends I spend time with and I can help what kind of music I listen to and what kind of movies I watch and what kinds of books I read. These are the things that will help produce the kinds of thoughts that I have.

How is your thought life? Is your mind filled with pure and virtuous things? Have you allowed your mind to be filled with the evil things? God is calling us to a higher standard than the world has—to purity in our thought life.

We Must Think about Positive Things.

Going one step further, Paul elevated the standard of Christian thinking above not thinking bad thoughts to always thinking good thoughts. Notice that Paul urges the Philippians to think about things that are, *"lovely . . . admirable . . . excellent . . . praiseworthy."* What Paul was saying is we must be constantly focusing our attention upon the good and not the bad around us.

Obviously, this is not an absolute statement. There are times when it is necessary to think about negative things. Paul wrote to the Corinthians and told them to discipline an immoral brother. Certainly the process of doing that was not necessarily pleasant. There are and will be times when we are forced to think about unpleasant things. However, in those times when we are not forced to think about such things, Paul encourages us to be thinking about the things that are good and honest and noble and upright.

The quickest way to spoil your ministry and ruin the joy of the Lord is to focus on the negative things around you. Focusing on the negative will have many serious results.

- *It will make you suspicious of others.* Negative people are always suspicious of other people, thinking that there is something sinister behind their actions.
- *It will drive your joy away.* If you are always suspicious of people and always thinking someone is trying to take advantage of you, there will be no joy in your life.
- *It will destroy your motivation.* If you have little joy in what you are doing and can see little positive coming out of it, your motivation will soon be destroyed.
- *It will create an attitude of superiority.* If all you see are problems, you will soon develop a paternalistic attitude or a "holier than thou"

attitude or some other attitude that encourages you to look down on other people.
- *It will destroy your ministry.* If you think so much about negative things, you will become so discouraged that you will be unable to do what God has called you to do.

I recognize there are a lot of negative things out there in the world. Although I have to think about those things like everyone else, I choose not to dwell on those things. Rather I choose to think about the good things that happen.

Recently I went with some friends to Akwanga for a time of fellowship. On the way, we had two confrontations with highway revenue collectors who stopped our vehicle with their nail boards, demanding an outrageous price for some transit permit. Because private vehicles are exempt from such things I refused to pay for it so we were delayed about an hour. We were quite angry about the whole thing. When we finally got to Akwanga, we explained what had caused our delay to our friends. For some time we continued to discuss this issue, speculating about the motivations of these people and complaining that the federal government is not controlling this kind of thing. After grumbling like this for a while, I made this announcement:

> Ladies and gentlemen, we are all familiar with what happened on the road this morning. I think we have said enough about it. These people have the ability to delay us and cost us time but we must refuse to allow them to spoil our time of fellowship. Therefore, I do not want to hear anything else about this incident. We do not have enough time to enjoy the fellowship with one another. Let us not spoil this time by thinking about those negative things.

I was very pleased with the way my colleagues responded. They were so conscientious about my speech that even when it came time to pray, they carefully crafted their prayers so as not to refer to that incident. I am convinced we have to make a deliberate choice at times that we will not allow ourselves to be sucked into negative thinking.

Those of you in administrative or decision-making positions have to be problem solvers. To be a problem solver, you have to even search for the negative. People come to you with problems regularly. If you are constantly bombarded with too many problems and do not stop occasionally and think about the good things, you will develop a negative and warped view of life.

One of my American missionary friends told me some years ago, "Danny, I've got to leave Nigeria." I had not been in Nigeria long and tried to convince him to stay. However, he said, "No, I am getting too cynical of everything. I find myself angry at Nigerians most of the time." He did not need to say more. It was indeed time for him to go.

I encourage you to watch the kinds of thoughts you allow yourselves to think. If you are constantly focusing on the negative, it will eventually destroy your ministry.

Three Young Missionary Couples

Three young American missionary couples had planned to come to Nigeria for several years. They went to seminary and missionary candidate school together. They were as well prepared as any missionary candidates could be. They came to Nigeria and were assigned to projects fairly close to one another. They saw each other often. I met all three couples during their first few months in Nigeria. I became concerned about one couple because almost all they could talk about was the negative. Everything was bad. The electricity did not work; the roads were bad; their helpers were dishonest; they could not get enough fuel. Although I had not been in the country very long, I could see real danger ahead. I was sure that when these young couples got together they were only talking about the negative.

About a year later I met one of these couples at the Kano airport. They informed me they were leaving and not coming back. What made this situation even sadder was that this was the last of the three couples to return home. In less than one year, three well qualified, fully financed missionary couples left the mission field. I am convinced the main reason for their leaving was their negative focus. As they shared their complaints and negative thoughts, these eventually destroyed their spirit and vision, and all the ministry they could have given to Nigeria was lost.

I know it is necessary at times to talk some of the garbage out of your soul. However, that must not be your focus.

How do you avoid getting in this endless cycle of negative thinking? I do not know of a guaranteed formula. However, there are times when you have to make a deliberate choice to think about positive things. And when I am forced to think about the negative things of life, I will often force myself to balance up those thoughts with positive things.

An Honest Groundnut Seller

When I first came to Jos, I was walking across the University of Jos campus one day. An hour later I passed by the same place and a young Muslim girl came running up to me. She said, "Oga, your money-o," and she handed me a 20-Naira note. She explained that when I had walked by earlier she had seen a 20-Naira bill drop from my pocket. She had picked it up and had been waiting for an hour for me to come back so she could give it to me.

Whenever I am tempted to think too much about the corruption and other evils of the world, I think about that incident and others like it and that helps bring negative things into perspective. Is every policeman corrupt? Do all students cheat? Is every stranger trying to manipulate you? Have we not experienced more positive things in life than negative things? Sometimes we have to deliberately force ourselves to think about those positive things.

Specifically what can we do to avoid negative thinking?

Avoid too much contact with negative people. I do not enjoy being around certain people, those people who are always pointing out the negative things in life.

Our organization has assigned several people to work in Port Harcourt over the years. Whenever I would orient these people, I would always tell them, "Be careful about spending too much time with the oil workers." Many of these oil workers see little good in Nigeria and nearly everything that comes out of their mouth is negative.

If you discover you are spending most of your time talking about negative things when you are around certain people, either deliberately try to change that or stay away from them. They will force you to think about negative things.

Remove music that does not honor Christ. I have become embarrassed by some of the American music that is played on our local radio stations. Some of it is so vulgar that it would not be allowed to play on radios in the US and yet it is played in Nigeria. If you are going to think pure and holy thoughts, you are going to have to remove this kind of vulgar and worldly music from your ears.

Do not read things that cause you to have bad thoughts. The world is filled with trashy books and magazines. But it is also filled with much good literature. Why should we spend our valuable time reading garbage when there are so many good things to read?

Refuse to watch movies that will encourage negative and sinful thoughts. Many Christians need to be much more discriminating in the kinds of movies they watch. It is a shame when we tolerate the most serious kinds of sinful behavior in our homes through the movies we watch. We must remember the eye gate is the most effective way of filling our minds with good or bad. A picture is worth a thousand words, whether good or bad.

There are also some positive things we should do.

Spend most of your time with godly people. Choose your friends carefully. Some people are always positive when you are around them. After your visit with them, you feel good and you look forward to being with them again. My mother taught me "birds of a feather flock together." We will become like the people we spend time with. Therefore, we must make a deliberate effort to spend time primarily with those who will encourage us not discourage us.

Fill your homes and rooms with beautiful pictures and other reminders of noble things. As I travel and sometimes stay with people who have teenagers, I am appalled at some of the pictures and posters they have on their walls. How can you think about holy things when the walls of your room are covered with pictures of unholy people?

A Widow's Sons All Become Sailors

I heard a preacher tell a story about a widow who raised six sons. She complained to her pastor that, contrary to her wishes, all of her sons joined the navy when they got old enough, leaving her alone. One day when the pastor visited her home, he understood. There in the living room was a huge beautiful picture of a ship out on the ocean plowing through the waves. The spray was coming over the bow and the scene was one of beauty and adventure. The picture was like a naval officer calling to those children all throughout their childhood. It was little wonder that these boys responded to that call when they were old enough.

Fill your mind with God's word. There are many good things in the world but we know that the Bible contains the purest truth of all. We should make sure that we are reading the Bible every day. A good way to keep wicked thoughts out of your mind is to memorize Scripture. I frequently keep little note cards in my pocket with a Scripture that has meant something to me so I can meditate on it while I am driving down the road or doing other things when my mind is not occupied.

Fill your life with positive activities. If you are busy doing good things —helping people, encouraging the depressed, supporting the weak, doing creative and positive things, you will have little time for thinking about evil things. Even teenagers can find many good things to do. I sang in a music group as a teenager. We were constantly busy either practicing or traveling. I participated in a lot of witnessing activities. When we went out doing such positive things, we returned with our minds filled with good experiences.

We Must Think about Jesus Christ

If there ever was a person who embodied the positive and wholesome things that Paul told us that we need to think about, it was Jesus Christ.

- Jesus is the embodiment of truth. He said, *"I am the way and the truth and the life"* (John 14:6).
- Jesus is the ultimate example of nobility. In his revelation John saw written on Jesus *"King of Kings and Lord of Lords"* (Revelation 19:16).
- Jesus was righteousness incarnate. A pagan soldier said about him, *"Surely this was a righteous man"* (Luke 23:47).
- Jesus was pure within and without. The Hebrew writer described Jesus to be *"holy, blameless, pure, set apart from sinners, exalted above the heavens"* (7:26).
- Jesus was not lovely in any physical sense (Isaiah 53:2) but he was a person with eyes *"like blazing fire, and on his head are many crowns"*

(Revelation 19:12). Jesus testified that he was *"the bright Morning star"* (22:16).
- Jesus is the most admired man throughout the history of the world. *"Therefore God exalted him to the highest place and gave him the name that is above every name, that at the name of Jesus every knee should bow, in heaven and on earth and under the earth"* (Philippians 2:9-10).
- Jesus is the greatest human example of excellence. Peter declared that Jesus had left us *"an example, that you should follow in his steps. 'He committed no sin, and no deceit was found in his mouth'"* (1 Peter 2:21-22).
- Jesus was the one that the angels in heaven bowed before and said, *"Worthy is the Lamb, who was slain, to receive power and wealth and wisdom and strength and honor and glory and praise!"* (Revelation 5:12).

Four verses before this powerful exhortation to think positive things, Paul wrote, *"Rejoice in the Lord always. I will say it again: Rejoice!"* (4:4). Rejoicing is one of the most positive things a person can do. In fact, in order to rejoice, you have to focus on something positive. What is it that is going to keep a person joyful? It is rejoicing *"in the Lord."*

There are 38 references to "Jesus" or "Christ" and another 10 references to "Lord" in the four chapters of Philippians. Many consider Philippians the epistle of joy. There is little wonder it is so joyful because it is so full of teachings about and references to Jesus. If we want to fill our minds full of positive thoughts, we must focus our attention on Jesus.

John Newton is most well known for his much loved hymn *Amazing Grace*. However, he has written another beautiful hymn in old European English that describes how thinking about Jesus filled him with blessing and joy and failing to think about Jesus filled him with gloom and depression.

How tedious and tasteless the hours
When Jesus no longer I see;
Sweet prospects, sweet birds, and sweet flowers,
Have all lost their sweetness to me;
The midsummer sun shines but dim,
The fields strive in vain to look gay;
But when I am happy in him,
December's as pleasant as May.

His name yields the richest perfume,
And sweeter than music his voice;
His presence disperses my gloom,
And makes all within me rejoice;
I should, were he always thus nigh,
Have nothing to wish or to fear;
No mortal so happy as I,
My summer would last all the year.

Content with beholding his face,
My all to his pleasure resigned,
No changes of season or place
Would make any change in my mind:
While blest with a sense of his love,
A palace a toy would appear;
And prisons would palaces prove,
If Jesus would dwell with me there.

Dear Lord, if indeed I am thine,
If thou art my sun and my song,
Say, why do I languish and pine?
And why are my winters so long?
O drive these dark clouds from my sky,
Thy soul cheering presence restore;

Or take me to thee up on high,
Where winter and clouds are no more.

Summary

Recently I read John 3:17 and even though I had read it many times, this time I saw something new. *"For God did not send his Son into the world to condemn the world, but to save the world through him."* The point I observed was that Jesus' purpose for coming to this world was not negative. Although Jesus' ministry had to address such negative things as sin, the focus of his work was not condemnation but salvation. It was not negative but positive.

The real heart of the Pharisee's belief and practice was condemnation. Their philosophy went something like this:

- We will point out your failures in life.
- Your sins and failures should activate your conscience.
- Your guilty conscience should force you to improve your behaviour.

Unfortunately, we still have some of this kind of legalistic condemnation today. The focus is on the negative, the rules and things we should not do. Jesus said he did not come to the world primarily to focus on condemnation. He came to focus on salvation which is holistic and positive.

You should think about some of these important questions:

- Where is the focus of your life?
- Can you only see the bad in the world or in your particular village or place of ministry?
- Do you see a lot more negative things where you minister than positive things?

- Are you constantly focusing on the negative or are you thinking about those things which are good and wholesome, admirable, lovely and excellent?
- Does your ministry focus more on condemnation than salvation?

CHAPTER 20

CONTENTMENT

(4:10-13)

Paul began this section by reflecting on the concern that the Philippians had shown for him. According to Paul, they had been concerned about him but had not been able to show it. However, Paul quickly added a statement lest the Philippians think he was hinting that they should do more for him.

> *I am not saying this because I am in need, for I have learned to be content whatever the circumstances. I know what it is to be in need, and I know what it is to have plenty. I have learned the secret of being content in any and every situation, whether well fed or hungry, whether living in plenty or in want. I can do everything through him who gives me strength.*
>
> —Phil. 4:11-13

Paul had learned to be content. How can a person be content? There are at least two possible ways:

Satisfy all your desires. Get everything you could possibly want. That would require unlimited wealth. Even if you had enough money to get anything you wanted, you would then have a desire for something money could not buy.

Someone asked a rich man how much money it would take to make him happy and he replied, "Just one more dollar." He was always just short of contentment because he always wanted just a little bit more. Therefore it is not likely you are going to be content by getting all you want.

Get rid of (or reduce) most of your desires. Socrates said, "If you want to make a man happy, add not to his possessions but take away from his desires." Though this statement may not be entirely true, it makes a point. Certainly there are genuine desires we have to fulfill. Paul had a desire to depart and be with Christ (Philippians 1:23). However, the truly contented person is one who has reduced his or her desires, particularly desires for non-essential things. If you do not have too many desires, then you will not often be disappointed because your desires are not fulfilled.

Most Westerners are products of a materialistic society, one that stresses acquiring, owning and using things. The commercial world is anxious for us to buy their products so they can make more money. It is difficult to really be content in this world. Most Africans have not been raised in quite the same way but the temptation, even in Africa, is to focus on material things. Paul, however, declared that he was content in every circumstance.

Content in Poverty

"I know what it is to be in need" (4:12). This was Paul's confession. The one who became the greatest missionary of all time had serious needs that were not met. In 2 Corinthians he outlined some of those needs.

Very few people in this world have everything they want so most of us think of ourselves as fitting into the category of the needy. According to some prosperity preachers, the believer should never have to make this negative confession: *"I know what it is to be in need."* Some of you have needs that are not being met. You do not know where you are going to get the money to take care of important needs. Some of you have unmet needs in your ministry. Are you willing to live in poverty if that is what God calls you to do?

Content in Abundance

"I know what it is to have plenty" (4:12). Very few of us would admit we are wealthy. However, wealth is relative. If you have more than you need, then you are wealthy by some standard.

Paul was mature enough—he knew what to do when he found himself in a surplus situation. I am confident that Paul never wasted that abundance that God gave him. He told us what we should do with any surplus money God gives us:

> *He who has been stealing must steal no longer, but must work, doing something useful with his own hands, that he may have something to share with those in need.*
> —Ephesians 4:28

God does not give us an abundance so that we can consume it on our own selfish desires. He gives us more than we need so we can share it with others.

I am saddened when I hear of preachers who think that by spending money lavishly they are somehow showing what a mighty God they serve. They are only showing they know little about the simplicity of Christ and demonstrate their ignorance about what it means to be a steward of God's resources.

Content in Changing Circumstances

"I have learned the secret of being content in any and every situation, whether well fed or hungry, whether living in plenty or in want." Most people live a fairly consistent life. However, Paul's life was one of constantly

changing circumstances. One day he was in the governor's mansion and the next he was in jail. One day he was preaching before huge crowds. The next day he was prohibited from even talking to anyone.

From Breakfast with the President to Public Transportation

In 2001 I had a private breakfast one morning with the president of Nigeria, President Obasanjo. We ate a lavish meal in Aso Rock. Twenty-four hours later, I was riding in a public transportation vehicle across Benin sitting beside people I did not know. The vehicle was so crowded that my back could not touch the back of the seat. Obviously I was a whole lot more content in the first situation than in the second. However, I was also happy to be in the crowded taxi because I was working on a new kind of ministry for our organization. And that filled me with amazing joy.

Have you learned to be content?

- You are not content when you are constantly worrying about your condition.
- You are not content if you are constantly complaining about the circumstances.
- You are not content when you are spending an inordinate amount of time trying to change the circumstances.

Contentment is relaxing in the sovereignty of God. Contentment is not laziness, sitting around just trusting the Lord that the dishes will be washed. However, a contented person recognizes that God is ultimately in control of our circumstances and is more than capable of changing them in his time and in his way. It is hard to fall into temptation when you are contented.

A Wonderful Business Opportunity

Some time ago, I received a phone call from a man who sounded like he had a Japanese accent. He said that he had met one of my students at a trade fair and my student had recommended that he contact me. He said that he represented a medical equipment company from Japan that needed to get some raw material from Nigeria. They used this material to make lenses for surgical microscopes. He said they had been getting this raw material from Iraq but due to the war, that source had dried up. They had learned this material was available in Nigeria. However, they also were aware of the reputation of Nigeria and they wanted someone they could trust to help them link up with the right person to secure the product.

I am always happy to help Nigeria. If this request could help Nigeria export something besides oil, I would be happy to help. I told him I knew nothing about this material but I would link him up with someone in our geology department. He kept calling, hinting at a lot of money to be made. They were looking for an agent and would pay him a 10 percent commission. However, I continued insisting that I was not a businessman and was not interested in his percentage. My only interest was to help the country. Eventually it became obvious that this whole thing was a 419 scam. Fortunately, I was never really in danger of getting sucked in because I was content with my circumstances. God has not called me to be involved in business. He has called me to preach and teach and write and help develop projects in Nigeria and I am perfectly happy to do that. When you are content there is much less temptation from the offers to make money.

Here are some questions for our consideration:

- Are you content with the house God has given you?
- Are you content with the ministry God has given you?

- Are you content with the ministry partners God has given you?
- Are you content with the compensation you are receiving for your work?
- Are you content with the circumstances in your life that are beyond your control?

When we relax and remain content in our circumstances rather than constantly trying to push ourselves to the top, we become ideal candidates for the grace of God and the joy of the Lord.

CHAPTER 21

GIVING

(4:14-19)

The church at Philippi was a church filled with joy. In fact, there is more stress placed on joy in Philippians than in any other epistle. Interestingly, the Philippian church was also the most generous church that Paul ever planted. Notice these comments in this section about giving;

> *Yet is was good of you to share in my troubles . . . not one church shared with me in the matter of giving and receiving, except you only; for even when I was in Thessalonica, you sent me aid again and again . . . I have received full payment and even more; I am amply supplied, now that I have received from Epaphroditus the gifts you sent. They are a fragrant offering, an acceptable sacrifice, pleasing to God.*
>
> —Phil. 4:15b-18

What do these statements teach us about giving?

Giving Is One of God's Means of Helping Needy People.

"Yet it was good of you to share in my troubles" (4:14a). In the Old Testament, farmers were instructed not to reap the corners of their fields so that the poor could glean something to eat.

Sometimes people have such serious needs that they cannot possibly meet them without some outside help. In the West, we have insurance, retirement and government welfare programs to help our continued independence of one another. However, in most places of the world, they still practice family and friend interdependence. They have to depend on one another in times of difficulty.

Galatians 6 has two statements only three verses apart that appear to be contradictory in the KJV.

- 6:2, *Bear ye one another's burdens* . . .
- 6:5, *For every man shall bear his own burden.*

What does this strange contradiction mean? Are we really supposed to bear our own burdens or are we supposed to bear the burdens of others? The issue is cleared up when we understand that Paul actually used two different Greek words here. The first word is *baros*, which was used of a ship's cargo. The second word is *phortion*, which was used of a soldier's pack. Although a soldier's pack was heavy and difficult to carry, a soldier could carry it. On the other hand, it would be practically impossible for one person to unload the cargo of a ship. So verse 5 means that each of us will have things to carry that are heavy. However, verse 2 means that we must have others help us carry burdens that are too heavy for us to carry.

We should not be ashamed to ask for help when we are carrying loads that are too heavy for us. And we should not hesitate to help people with their loads when it is obvious they are too heavy to carry. I believe it is more honoring to God to help one another in times of need than to trust entirely on our own independence and personal reserves.

Shortly after becoming a pastor, a friend gave me a cheque for $100. Because I had been in school many years, we had been forced to live very simply. Any extra money was usually for a specific purpose. Since we did not have any particular need at that time, I was puzzled about why I had received it. Shortly after that my sister came to see us with a very sad story. They had recently sold their car, but the cheque was bad. They had been counting on that money to meet some obligations so they were very needy. I knew instantly why God had given me that money. He had given it so that I could give it to my sister in her time of need. A few weeks later the police recovered the vehicle. My sister was able to sell the car and they sent me back the $100. It just so happened that that was the time when our last baby, Laura, was born and now we were in need of money. I have always marveled at how God took that same one hundred dollars and used it to meet two important needs.

Giving Is One of God's Means of Financing His Work

"For even when I was in Thessalonica, you sent me aid again and again when I was in need" (4:16). Paul was in Thessalonica doing the Lord's work and the method God chose to finance his project was through the gifts of Christians. This was true throughout the Bible. The tabernacle and later the temple were built with the sacrificial gifts of God's people.

Most Christian workers are able to feed their families because someone donates money to the church which provides them with their income. Thus, those who are involved in Christian ministry understand very well the importance of giving. It is my advice that Christian workers should not only be recipients of giving but also be givers also. Perhaps those who are involved in full time Christian ministry do not have as much to give as someone else, but their gifts will help meet the needs of others as the gifts of others meet their needs.

Giving Is Pleasing to God

"They [the gifts] *are a fragrant offering, an acceptable sacrifice, pleasing to God"* (4:18a). All of us are anxious to please our superiors and important people. Although understanding the emotions of God is beyond my ability to comprehend, according to this passage, one of the things that makes God happy is when you give to one another.

Giving Is a Means of God Giving Back to Us

Paul made an amazing statement at the close of this section on giving. *"And my God will meet all your needs according to his glorious riches in Christ Jesus"* (4:19). There is something about giving that stimulates others to give. When we give to others, very often others will give back to us.

Daniel Learns a Lesson about Giving

When my son Daniel was six years old, he said, "Daddy, I want to help you with your computer." I had been talking for some weeks about buying a computer and the children knew that we could not buy it unless we had the money so we had been saving money to buy it. Daniel handed me seven cents. I thanked him sincerely. About 3 minutes later, he returned to my office, "Daddy, look what I found." He had removed the cushions from the couch probably to jump up and down on them and there were three dimes and three pennies, 33 cents. I saw an opportunity to teach him about giving so I lined up the seven cents he had given to me on one side and his new 33 cents on the other side and asked, "Daniel, which would you rather have, the seven cents or the 33 cents?" He chose the 33 cents. I then told him that God had rewarded him with 33 cents because of his gift of seven cents. Later he checked all the chairs in the house and found two quarters, so now he had 83 cents.

Here is another part of the story: After he was asleep, I slipped into his room and put his seven cents back in his little bank. I really did not need his money but it made me feel very good that he was willing to give it. As a result of freely giving seven cents, he had gotten:

- a new 83 cents
- his original 7 cents
- the good feeling of giving
- an important lesson about giving

God must look at us in a similar way. He really does not need our money but it makes him feel good when we give to him or others. I am sure he creates interesting ways to give back our investment to us with wonderful interest.

When we give, God always gives back but not necessarily in kind. You may give money but he will give you back energy. You may give time and he will give back joy. You may give him worship and he gives you health.

Giving Is a Great Source of Joy

This truth is not exactly taught in this paragraph but it is taught and implied throughout the epistle. It is no wonder that the most giving church Paul wrote to was also the most joyful church.

Do you want your life to be filled with joy? Give to God and his people. There may be a certain amount of good feeling in receiving something that you have needed or looked forward to getting for a long time. However, the real joy in this world is the joy of giving.

My mother is the greatest giver I know. She seems to get the greatest joy out of giving. As long as my father was alive, his salary and later his pension was all that they needed to live on. My mother was a full time wife and mother so did not work out of the home. However, she has written several books that she would sell and that would generate a little money. Her relatives and friends would sometimes give her money for her birthday or as a Christmas gift. That gave her some personal money that she could give away to the next needy person or the next Christian ministry that came along. I can hardly remember a time when she spent "her" money on herself. It was always something that she gave away to other people.

The real application of this truth is to the members of the Philippian Church who were giving money to support Paul's work. However, there is also an application to missionaries, Christian workers and ordinary Christians. All God's people must give.

- Are you a giving person?
- Are you a person who thinks about the needs of others?
- Are you a person who gets a lot of joy out of giving?

Most people love Philippians 4:19, *"And my God will meet all your needs according to his glorious riches in Christ Jesus."* We quote that verse when we have a need. However, we need to make sure we understand the context of this passage as well. Note the statements that are made about the Philippians in the immediate preceding context:

- *"not one church shared with me in the matter of giving and receiving, except you only"* (4:15)
- *"you sent me aid again and again when I was in need"* (4:16)
- *"I have received from Epaphroditus the gifts you sent"* (4:18)

The Philippians were giving people. They had been faithful and sacrificial in giving to meet Paul's needs and now Paul promised them that God would also meet their needs. The point is this: If we are generous in using our resources to meet the needs of others, God will be faithful to meet all of our needs as well.

CHAPTER 22

CONCLUSION

The Book of Philippians is a small book with a big message. It is a snapshot of a young "missions" church that was probably not more than 10 years old when Paul wrote this letter to them. The church had many of the typical problems and blessing that many of our modern churches have. However, the Philippian church had one other important thing in their favor. They were deeply loved and cared for by the Apostle Paul. He loved them so much that he wrote this thoughtful epistle to encourage, correct and bless. And his writings to this young church are just as applicable and helpful to us today as they were to the Philippians 2000 years ago.

It is my prayer that the truths of Philippians will be a part of your church and, even more importantly, a part of your life. I will conclude this book by paraphrasing one of the statements that Jesus gave us: "I pray that you will know the truths found in Philippians and these truths will set you free."

www.ingramcontent.com/pod-product-compliance
Lightning Source LLC
Chambersburg PA
CBHW061430040426
42450CB00007B/987